The Temper of Western Europe

Crane Brinton

The Temper
of Western Europe

Harvard University Press

Cambridge, Massachusetts

1953

To my friends in

Charlottesville

Prefatory Note

This book is an expansion of the James W. Richard Lectures in History delivered at the University of Virginia on April 21, 22, and 23, 1953. I wish to thank the authorities at the University for giving me this early opportunity, after my return from Europe, to organize my impressions of the temper of Western Europeans. I must thank also Mr. Thomas J. Wilson, Director of the Harvard University Press, and his staff for their collaboration in the task of bringing out this book with a speed imposed by the subject but taxing severely the sound traditions of university publishing. I thank once more my secretary, Miss Elizabeth F. Hoxie, for her care in the preparation of the manuscript.

Crane Brinton

Peacham, Vermont
August 20, 1953

Contents

I. WESTERN EUROPE: DYING OR LIVING? 1

 The Prophets of Doom 1

 On Method, Briefly 7

II. THE URGENT PRESENT 13

 The Extent of Western Europe 13

 A Traveler's Glimpse 17

 The Material Basis 23

III. THE PERSISTENT PAST 47

 Rebuilding 47

 Nationalism 49

 Political Forms 54

 The Persistent Social Structure 61

 The Survival of Individualism 68

IV. THE POSSIBLE FUTURE 76

 European Union 76

 The Economic Future 86

 The Spirit of Western Europe 97

Western Europe: Dying or Living?

The Prophets of Doom

"The period through which we are living presents itself as one of unmitigated confusion and disintegration . . . "

"We can assert with some confidence that our own period is one of decline; that the standards of culture are lower than they were fifty years ago; and that the evidences of this decline are visible in every department of human activity."

"For myself, and I was not alone, all the conscious and recollected years of my life have been lived to this day under the heavy threat of world catastrophe, and most of the energies of my mind and spirit have been spent in the effort to grasp the meaning of these threats, to trace them to their sources and to understand the logic of this majestic and terrible failure of the life of man in the Western World."

To these wails from Lewis Mumford, T. S. Eliot, and Katherine Anne Porter, which Mr. William Shirer uses as an epigraph for his own wake over the corpse of Europe, *Midcentury Journey*, one may add dozens from Mr. Shirer's book alone. The star of France is waning; in Germany the Master Race is at it again; there will probably not always be an England. Mr. Shirer's plane did but touch down at the great—and lively—Shannon airport. The plane stayed long enough, however, to allow Mr. Shirer to confirm his natural feeling that something was wrong in Ireland. "Now that its great political struggle against Britain had been won there was every reason to believe that a free and independent Ireland would flower as never before.

"But somehow, even after a new constitution, hammered out by De Valera in 1937, proclaimed Ireland to be a sovereign, independent, democratic state, cutting off almost the last slender ties with the British Commonwealth and king and re-establishing the old Gaelic name of Eire, and even after the last threads of connection were severed and Eire became, on Easter Monday, April 18, 1949, 'the Republic of Ireland,' the dream faded, the great objectives were lost sight of and Ireland struck even such a sympathetic observer as this one as a community whose vision had narrowed, a parochial place preoccupied with pettiness, content to remove itself from the major currents of Western life and thought, intent on censoring good books and denying many of its greatest writers. Freedom, by some queer quirk of reversal, appeared to have dulled the fine creativeness of a poetic and imaginative people."

Mr. Arthur Koestler is an even gloomier witness. His *Age of Longing* is a novel of postwar Western Europe, with the scene for the most part in Paris and with a thoroughly modern international cast of weak, unhappy, and frustrated characters, interspersed with a few stronger but even more depraved ones. There is a Communist of course who knows where he is going—and it is a most unpleasant place. We need not concern ourselves with the details of the story. One character, however, symbolizes nicely Mr. Koestler's feeling of hopelessness. This is an aged French aristocrat, a bundle of nastiness. He is full of obsessions which, since his creator is Mr. Koestler, spill over into symbols of our present distress. He has a special obsession about the prostate gland, and the France, indeed the whole West, of his time comes out as a swollen prostate. This is indeed a neat figure of speech. In one unpleasant symbol Mr. Koestler combines the worst he can feel about our times: old age and impotence and disease. No therapy, not even surgery, will save this French aristocrat and the world he symbolizes.

As a final exhibit I should like to add an excerpt from a private letter from a most sensitive and distinguished literary friend of mine, an American in Paris: "Paris, even in its old age is exciting—one thinks of Ninon de Lenclos and Mistinguette." Now when I came back to Paris in the winter of 1952–1953 for the first time since 1944, I too found it exciting; but since I was engaged in driving a car across the city, I did not think of Mistinguette or of Ninon de Lenclos. Indeed, in the midst of the fury of motor traffic in those age-old streets (Baron Haussmann, who built so many of them, died about sixty years ago) I confess I did not even give any thought to the metaphor of age and decay, which seems to obsess so many contemporary Americans reporting on Western Europe; and if the image of death did cross my mind, it was not a tragic Toynbean collapse of a great society that worried me, but a simple vulgar fear for my own safety in traffic at least as dense as in the United States, and, most Americans feel, even wilder.

Now I must warn the reader that by temperament and training I am disposed to doubt the accuracy of reports like those I have just cited. By temperament I am probably a kind of optimist. At least I believe that there is a hard resisting core of human nature which will stand much more eroding from the forces of evil than it has had even in these devilish times. By training I am a historian, and in particular a historian of revolutions in the modern West. In a revolution the commentators, and indeed often the participants, are inclined to announce that everything that was has been destroyed, that everything that is has become magically new. The hurricane has blown down all the trees; we've got to plant new ones—full-grown ones if possible. But if you will look carefully at revolutions in the past, you will discover some very tall oaks, to say nothing of a thicket of less imposing vegetation, standing there after the winds have done their worst. In the France of 1794, after five years of increasing revolutionary violence, you will find not only the thicket of French family relations growing as before, but you will find at least one sturdy oak of the *ancien régime,* the power of the central government, standing stronger than ever in its new growth.

I was, then, in advance skeptical of the diagnosis of fatal disease in the collectivity of postwar Western Europe, skeptical of metaphors of all-destroying storms, even though—perhaps, just because—they came from such distinguished intellectuals as Mr. Koestler and Mr. Shirer. Six months of travel in Britain, France, Switzerland, and Spain in the second half of 1952 confirmed me in my belief that—to put it mildly—the condition of Western Europe is not as bad as it is generally believed to be in this country. This book is an effort to justify and explain that belief.

There is indeed a certain arrogance in the famous phrase of the historian Leopold von Ranke, a phrase which nevertheless the most relativistic of historians would hardly deny in his heart: *er will bloss erzeigen, wie es eigentlich gewesen* —he (the historian) will merely show how it really was. But there is an arrogance, too, in the writer of the opposite sort who feels that his own emotional responses to the universe are somehow in themselves the best version of how it really is. I do indeed think that I have in this book given a truer, a more accurate account of the temper of Western Europe in our times than has, for one instance, Mr. Shirer in his *Midcentury Journey.*

I did not, of course, go to Europe with an open mind—not at any rate open in the sense in which naïve common sense seems to think of the objective scientist's mind. I did not go without guiding predispositions, without even tentative answers to tentative questions. In short, I did not go with an empty mind. I went, needled no doubt by reading men like Mr. Koestler, quite convinced that I should find more signs of life in Western Europe than of death, more signs that men and women were struggling bravely and not altogether unsuccessfully against very grave difficulties indeed than signs that they were lapsing into despairing apathy or struggling feverishly and vainly like a sick person turning from side to side—from Left to Right—in hopeless sickness. I found substantially what I expected to find, as, quite clearly, did Mr. Shirer.

What marks objective thinking, however, is not absence of expectations or even, if you like, of conclusions made in advance, but a willingness to revise those conclusions if observation and experiment fail to confirm them. I trust that if I had found in Europe that my observations, the "facts of the case," showed in the balance that my anticipations had been wrong, showed that Europe was in as bad a way—well, in almost as bad a way—as these writers I quote have said

it was, I should have had the courage to revise my conclusions. Actually I found Western Europe, as far as I could
pretend to judge its temper as a whole, just a shade better
than I had expected to find it. But objectivity in the study
of human relations is very difficult to attain, far more difficult than in the natural sciences, where the "is" and the
"ought to be"—or even the "I want it to be"—get so much
less in each other's way than in the study of human relations. Take this book, if you must, as no more than an emotional antithesis to the thesis of the prophets of doom and
the bellyaching intellectuals.

Finally, I have not interviewed the great in those countries of Western Europe we visited, nor, in any formal
sense, in the sense meant by either newspaper reporter or
pollers of public opinion when they conduct an interview,
have I interviewed ordinary West Europeans. We traveled
quite frankly for pleasure; and indeed it seems to me no small
item on the side of the thesis that Western Europe is not
hopelessly sunk in despair and decay that travel for pleasure
there should be quite possible. The dollar is of course an
advantage; but not even in Spain, which boasts its cheapness
for the American tourist, has the dollar today the shocking
advantage over local currency it had in countries like Austria right after the war of 1914–1918. In the course of such
normal travel I saw and talked informally with a great many
people, by no means all of them engaged in the business of
catering to the traveler; I saw many of my old friends in
Britain and in France, friends for the most part in academic
life, and not inclined to undue optimism in these days. I
sampled the newspaper and periodical press in each country, neglecting neither Left nor Right. I had, as a backlog,
some seven years all told of residence and travel in Europe,

mostly in Western Europe, extending at intervals from 1919 to the present, and including two years of residence in London and Paris during the last war. Out of these materials, and the reading of much of the work of my fellow commentators on Europe and the modern world, and with the temperament and the training I have tried to make clear to the reader, I have made this book.

On Method, Briefly

It is certainly presumptuous to attempt to analyze the state of mind, the temper, of some three hundred million people in the Western Europe of today. Even the most confident maker of generalizations must occasionally be disturbed by the leaps in the dark his mind has to make when he works up his incomplete supply of facts—no matter how big it is, it can never in matters of this sort be complete—into general propositions. Especially in the social sciences, one ought not to be too harsh on the researcher, naïve though he may be, who sticks to his little pile of carefully assayed facts and refuses to generalize. He also serves, and in this world where the crusader (who is inevitably a generalizer of sorts) has so much to crusade for and against, it seems a waste of time and energy to crusade against the Ph.D. and kindred research, even though it is devoted to such subjects as a statistical analysis of the reading habits of eight-year-olds in Buncombe County or of learning-response among a selected group of hamsters.

For we shall always have plenty of generalizers. Indeed, the very researchers who refuse to generalize about their own work will probably feel quite confident that the big trouble with contemporary France is the lack of a two-party system like ours and Britain's. We must make generalizations, even about Western Europe, which has not the political structure of a nation-state like France or Great Britain, which is, indeed, a comprehensible group or a whole only in the much less obvious and concrete sense of sharing a certain cultural tradition. Something more than the usual semantic grace with which it is now the fashion to approach problems like the one we are concerned with here is surely necessary. For men like Mr. Shirer and Mr. Koestler are serious, honest, and most intelligent thinkers, men who have had a long experience of the Western Europe they write about. At the very least, before we attempt to criticize their conclusions, we must make some attempt to understand how they came to them, why they omitted what seem to us quite obvious and pertinent "facts," why they weave other "facts" into a distorted pattern of generalization.

The easy and really quite unavoidable thing to say is that these prophets of doom are intellectuals. Now "intellectual" is a thoroughly bad term, rousing from the start all those hindrances to understanding the semanticist deplores. But it is better than the revealing vulgarisms, from "high-brow" to "long-hair" and "egghead," Americans have coined for it, and it is better than awkward if more accurate phrases like "one whose main occupation, or at least main avocation, is writing, teaching, preaching, acting, or the practice of the fine arts." The audience for these active intellectuals I should call the "intellectual classes." I like neither term, but I am at a loss for better ones. I hope that I am trying to use these terms neither in abuse nor in praise. Most of my readers, surely, are themselves intellectuals.

Now when he is confronted with a most involved problem such as that of describing the state of contemporary Western Europe, the contemporary intellectual if he belongs to the fashionable school of prophets of doom tends to omit certain facts and emphasize certain other facts. My literary correspondent, for example, emphasizes that Paris is an *old* city. So it is. It first appears in written history almost exactly two thousand years ago as Lutetia Parisiorum. Actually archaeology does not as yet push it back much further, but two thousand years is good enough for "old." Yet surely the overwhelming majority of the artifacts that make up Paris in 1953—the streets, sidewalks, buildings, sewers, lights, the rest of the public utilities, parks, all taken together—are no older than such artifacts in our American cities. One may guess that at least three quarters of the urban agglomeration we call Paris is less than seventy years old. You have to look hard in Paris to find the Middle Ages, and look very hard to find Lutetia Parisiorum. In some obvious and surely not unimportant respects Paris is a "young" city. This my correspondent does not say, not because he does not know it to be true, but because he is not thinking in terms that make such facts pertinent to his purposes.

I do not intend to let this excursion into what is really the enormous and most important subject of the sociology of knowledge get out of hand, and quite bury the main purpose of this book. But I may suggest that a carefully balanced analysis of what can justly be called "old" and what "new" in a city or a society is likely to turn out so complicated, so much a matter of delicate shadings, that the reader gets confused. He finds the analysis dull. And the intellectual, quite laudably, hates to be dull. A complete account of how the thinker's "purposes" affect his analysis would of course be a sociology of knowledge in itself. But I do wish to bring out two habits of mind of the modern intellectual which I think are of special importance in distorting his account of matters that do directly concern this study.

Let me start with a concrete instance, which I hope will turn out to be more pertinent to our purpose than it may at first seem to be. There is in the forest wilderness of Essex County, Vermont, a small body of water known as South America Pond, to which I once struggled through the black flies. The limited view one gets from the edge I reached does not suggest that the name makes any sense; but on the map the pond does look exactly the way South America looks—*on the map*. It has that familiar shape, bulge of Brazil and all. But only a generation brought up on school geographies could have so christened the pond. Had Samuel de Champlain himself penetrated to that part of the state he is said to have been responsible for naming from its Green Mountains, he could hardly have thought of the name South America Pond. One may say that in a very limited sense the name fits, though in most of what strikes an observer—the physiographic setting, the flora, the fauna —there is no relation whatever to South America. What actually are associated in this limited valid relation are sym-bols—abstractions if you don't mind—not by any means fresh, immediate sense-data, the things one ordinarily no-tices in New England ponds. Anyone who gathered from the name that there are llamas grazing on the banks of South America Pond, or that balsa-log craft float on its surface, would be very wrong indeed.

What I am trying to illustrate thus laboriously is merely the fact that with the great expansion of what has to go into our minds about the modern world, an expansion without which we could not live at all in this world, a great deal of our thinking has to be done in terms of relating symbols to other symbols, abstractions to other abstractions. But this useful and indeed necessary kind of thinking carries with it a grave danger: that it will go on indefinitely, symbol breeding symbol, without the necessary refreshing return of the mind to the directness of sense-experience. My correspondent, his mind full of French literature and history, was no doubt justified in linking the symbol "Ninon de Lenclos" with the symbol "Paris"—but only in a very limited sense. No one who looks at Paris with his eyes instead of his literary memories and preconceptions would see it first as an aged courtesan—nor even, actually, as a young one. Paris is indeed interested in sex, but by no means obsessed with it. For Paris as for the rest of France, sex is too important to be an obsession.

The second distorting habit of mind I want to mention is much more familiar to us in these days when everyone is a psychologist. It is the inevitable coloring our emotions give to our thinking, a coloring that goes on reproducing itself, even intensifying itself. Change awakens and stimulates our emotions; it takes an effort of the mind to keep hold on what persists, maintains itself. Disaster seems to call for adjectives like "complete," "total," "unparalleled"; anything less would mark one as insensitive. Disaster can indeed be total for the individual, but here on earth, very rarely indeed for the group. When Mr. Shirer writes that the Europe he first came to in 1925 "no longer existed" in 1950, he not merely makes a statement that is true only at a certain level of abstraction, true *with respect to* unstated conditions; he also gets the pleasure—I think it *must* be a pleasure for these prophets of doom—of letting his emotions well up freely.

We must not, however, yield to the Hegel that lurks within us all and try to get at the truth by asserting the exact opposite of these gloomy views. Even in the hands of masters of paradox like Bernard Shaw and Gilbert Chesterton, the technique of maintaining that what benighted ordinary people take to be black is really shining white can get a little wearing. A good many experienced people think and feel that Europe is in a bad way, and the very existence of this opinion must for us be one of the facts of life. Some academic devil in me does tempt me to defend the paradox that the United States, not Western Europe, is old. There is a good start in the statement, true within definable limits, that in a formal sense ours is the oldest political constitution of the major states of Western society. The United States is as a formal state older than the Fourth French Republic, older than the West German or the Italian Republics; it is older than the present British semisocialist state. Or, if you like to think of Britain in terms of Alfred the Great and Magna Carta, you will also have to think of the United States in those terms. There is a more dubious follow-up in Mr. Stuart Hughes's feeling that the United States is somehow a kind of Byzantium, a society born old. I shall withstand the temptation, however, to make ours an "old" country too, and seek nothing more spectacular than a balanced account of the state of contemporary Western Europe.

II

The Urgent Present

The term "Western Europe," which used to have chiefly
a geographical connotation, has since 1945 taken on political
and indeed moral connotations. We all use it, quite conscientiously, where in the old days we should simply have
written "Europe" and let it go at that. It is true that the
more than merely geographical factors that distinguish
Western from Eastern Europe have existed for many years.
They were not created, though they were certainly sharp-
ened, by the events of the postwar years. Men debated
whether Russia really belonged in Europe long before Yalta
and Potsdam. But the Iron Curtain is no mere metaphor.
Whether it divides essentially kindred if at present alienated
peoples, or whether it divides peoples of irreconcilably
opposed fundamental cultures—whether, in short, it is like
a Mason and Dixon's line in our own ante-bellum days or
like the historically shifting but very definite line that
divides Christian and Mohammedan cultures from the sev-
enth century on—it is now a very real line. The metaphor
of the curtain is apt. There is indeed a curtain, which can be
raised or lowered a bit, and no solid wall.

It runs, roughly, north and south along a line from the
Elbe to the head of the Adriatic Sea, and then east and west

to the Turco-Bulgarian frontier on the Black Sea. Like most such lines, it has its anomalies. Yugoslavia is for most purposes, though a Communist state, on the western side of the curtain; little Albania, though fronting on the Adriatic, is quite clearly on the eastern side. It has the great anomaly, that since in common language we talk of "Western Europe" as synonymous with "Europe outside the Iron Curtain," Western Europe has to stand for Southern and even Southeastern Europe, for the Iberian Peninsula, Italy, Greece, and Turkey. To get matters straight, we may list the "sovereign states" on the western, on "our" side of the curtain, with their populations and areas in round figures.

Table 1. Population and Area

	Population	Area in square miles
Great Britain	50,000,000	94,000
Republic of Ireland	3,000,000	27,000
France	42,000,000	213,000
Belgium	9,000,000	12,000
Luxembourg	300,000	1,000
Netherlands	10,000,000	16,000
Norway	3,000,000	125,000
Sweden	7,000,000	173,000
Denmark	4,000,000	17,000
West Germany	49,000,000	95,000
Switzerland	5,000,000	16,000
Portugal	9,000,000	35,000
Spain	29,000,000	196,000
Italy	47,000,000	116,000
Greece	8,000,000	50,000
Turkey	21,000,000	297,000
Total	296,300,000	1,483,000

These are rough figures, for the most part estimates made by statisticians of the United Nations for the early 1950's. They do not show the whole strength of these nations, for *as of the present* Britain, France, Belgium, and Portugal have territories overseas still tied to them by political and economic ties of varied degrees of closeness, and the Netherlands and Spain have small fragments left of their once-great overseas empires. It is not the province of this book to take up directly the complex question of the present and future of "colonialism." It is quite possible that in the long run, even in the fairly short run as history goes, European colonialism is doomed. But here, as so often when impatient prophets speak of "doom" for a politico-economic system, they take the word for the deed. Indo-China, for instance, is now almost certainly rather a liability than an asset to metropolitan France. But taking the whole network of relations gathered under the term "Europe overseas," from the tenuous bonds that hold South Africa in the British Commonwealth of Nations to the old-fashioned colonial dependence of Belgian Congo on Belgium, it is still true that overseas territories are an important factor in the total strength of Western Europe, a factor of major importance should there break out shortly a world war between coalitions headed respectively by the United States and Russia. Should such a war between the whole of the non-Communist and the whole of the Communist world break out, our side would have, in spite of the presence of thickly populated China on the Communist side, a very great advantage in population, area, and total material resources.

Our main concern in this study, however, is Western Europe itself. In the broad sense which includes the sixteen countries above listed, Western Europe has some 300,000,-000 inhabitants and 1,500,000 square miles. The USSR had in 1947, by their own government estimate to the United Nations, 193,000,000 inhabitants and 8,500,000 square miles; the United States in 1953 had just 160,000,000 in-

habitants and some 3,000,000 square miles. We shall, however, in this study be more directly concerned with the
heart of Western Europe, that part more clearly indicated
by the old geographical term "Northwestern Europe"—that
is, Great Britain, France, West Germany, and the smaller
countries of Scandinavia, "Benelux" (shorthand for Belgium, the Netherlands, and Luxembourg), Ireland, and
Switzerland. Recent events have linked Italy closely to this
area, as—at least until very recently—they have tended to
divide Spain from it. The five centuries since the great
period of geographical explorations of the fifteenth and six-
teenth centuries have made this region the richest, most
industrialized and most populous part of Europe, its heart-
land. It was not always such, and we should be usurping the
role of the prophet were we to assert that it always will be
such. For the present, however, these countries are a very
great part of Western society and civilization. Taken together these eleven countries have a total population somewhat greater than that of either the USSR (without its
satellites) or the United States.

But can they be realistically "taken together"? They are
still, in spite of the Schuman Plan, the North Atlantic
Treaty Organization, the Council of Europe, and the
United Nations, eleven independent "sovereign" nations.
Their past, even their very recent past, has seen them at war
in a great variety of combinations. Some of the great—one
almost said "classic"—antagonisms between human groups,
that between the Germans and the French, that between the
Irish and the English, and that—by no means ended though
the two have not formally fought in a declared war one
against the other since 1815—between the French and the
British, have grown up in this small area. One of our main

tasks in this book must be to examine the extent to which close political and economic coöperation, perhaps even a degree of actual union, is likely or possible in this Western Europe of the mid-twentieth century. But from the very start of our inquiry we must be warned against the over-simple formula "either–or." The problem of the 1950's is not one of either complete union of Western Europe or complete disintegration of Western Europe. It is rather how great a degree of the much-needed coöperation between the states of Western Europe is consistent with the actual state of mind—and body—of their peoples.

A Traveler's Glimpse

On the surface certainly the traveler in the heartlands of Western Europe, if he is not too bemused by the pre-conception that he is watching the death throes of a civilization, sees much to remind him that he is in one of the regions of the world where many men live well materially. The standard of municipal housekeeping is high, lower perhaps in France than in England or in Switzerland. But the back streets of Paris are still cleaner than the back streets of New York, and the post offices in smaller French towns are no more dismal than those in ours used to be before the New Deal muralists and architects brightened them up. The standard of domestic housekeeping remains high, higher in the poorer urban areas, in terms of what meets the traveler's eye, than in corresponding areas in this country.

The Golden Arrow still shoots at a dizzy speed across the plains of northern France, the Flying Scotsman still flies, its dining-car service a bit reduced in elegance perhaps, but no more than is fitting for the railroads of a social democracy. In Mayfair the hundreds of luxury shops make seductive displays, still with that touch unique to London that makes them even more seductive for the male customer than for the female. In Paris the *haute couture* flourishes. And neither in London nor in Paris does it appear that all the buyers are American. In French provincial towns the windows of *patisseries* and *charcuteries* are as full as ever of good things, so full that you know that ordinary Frenchmen must somehow find the francs for their *baba au rhum* and their *galantine de volaille*. No doubt the francs thus spent on delicacies cannot usually be stretched to cover electric blankets and television sets. It is indeed true that it is easy to convert to the uses of modern war factories making electrical gadgets, and quite impossible to so convert small shops making pastry, or even larger ones canning *pâté de foie gras*. It may be that the French, in thus preferring delicate foods to the products of the assembly line are, in a sense not meant by the coiners of the adage, digging their graves with their teeth. But somehow one hopes not.

No one could miss in England or France the scars of the last war, and they are of course even more visible in Western Germany, where I have not been since the war. Yet here again the eye will see what the heart wants and the mind expects. If you look for evidence that proves the last war so destructive that another war must destroy the physical basis of life where it is fought, you can find it, in London around St. Paul's, in the heart of Rouen or Beauvais and everywhere in Berlin. If you just look, however, you will see surprisingly little that will remind you of the horrors of war. The countryside has everywhere come back to its normal high state of cultivation. Indeed, this last war was so much a war of movement that almost nowhere did

the countryside suffer the intensified destruction of the top-
soil it suffered in 1914–1918 along the line of trench fighting. The traveler who knew his England even so recently
as the 1920's will indeed see a revolutionary change, but it
is not quite the kind of change that suggests death and decay. They really are using, to grow grain, sugar beets, and
the inevitable potato, those lovely hedged green fields
which before the war seemed to a foreign layman's eye
chiefly devoted to forming a fit setting for the horseback
pursuit of the fox.

They are, in spite of the demands of rearmament, rebuilding, and on a vast scale. The hopeful modernist plan-
ner must be for the most part disappointed in the results.
In England and in France at least, they have not avoided
stringing together long lines of houses which, if they are
not now quite as ugly as the semidetached villas of the Victorians and the Edwardians, look as though in fifty years they
may seem even uglier. But they have what even Americans
would consider the modern conveniences; they are com-
fortable. There is of course almost everywhere a continuing
crisis in housing. But this crisis is by no means wholly due
to the destruction caused by war. It is due quite as much to
a phenomenon we shall return to later, a phenomenon which
surely suggests life rather than death. There are several
million children in Western Europe who according to the
demographic experts of the 1930's just have no business
being there. Prosperous Western Europeans, like Americans, are having more babies.

There are those, both Americans and Europeans, who
maintain that people in Western Europe are unhappy, and
look it. M. Jean-Paul Sartre thinks that the French working-
man, beaten by his natural enemies, his employers, cheated

of the great hopes of the Liberation, has resigned himself to despair. A long time ago, in the most golden of golden ages, a Yankee intellectual, who was very Yankee and very intellectual, remarked that most men lead lives of quiet desperation. Thoreau's statement is not one that can be readily verified by the social scientist or even by the man of common sense. Noisy desperation, like that of M. Sartre, you can indeed verify quite easily; but quiet desperation by its very nature can be verified only in the intimacy of personal relations. I doubt whether M. Sartre has this intimate relationship with any of the workers whose cause he champions, any more than had poor old Wordsworth with the peasants he wrote about so touchingly. One of my good academic friends in Paris, forced by slender retirement pay to live in a working-class quarter, remarked to me that the workers in his neighborhood were said to be crowded ten in a room; but he admitted that since he is a bourgeois intellectual, he does not really mix with his neighbors. He had never actually *seen* them housed ten in a room—never, in fact, looked personally into their housing. As far as the superficial observation of a foreign traveler can go, I can only say that not even in Spain, where the poor really are poor and numerous, did I gather from the looks of the people that they were in either noisy or quiet desperation. The children, indeed, looked almost happy, as well as healthy, but this is perhaps an adult delusion.

Though again the social scientist has no really effective means of measuring such things, we all do register subjectively some comparative impressions of the feelings of the crowd. One of the favorite comparisons, which I suppose most of us have indulged in at one time or another, is that of the looks of our fellow passengers in subways,

buses, trams. Here I am hopelessly conventional. I find a
New York subway crowd the most harried, unhappy of
crowds, and in their midst I come almost to believe that
Thoreau was right about human beings. I find contemporary London and Paris subway crowds much less harried
in appearance, and provincial busloads in Western Europe
sometimes almost merry.

The traveler in Western Europe who knew the region
before war broke out in 1939 will indeed be struck with one
conspicuous difference from the old days, a difference re-
flecting the big facts the historian and the commentator
chronicle. Englishmen, before 1939 and even more before
1914 a more important element in the prosperity of the
great continental tourist industry than were the free-spend-
ing Americans of legend, are certainly not traveling the
way they used to. Their government, whether Labour or
Tory, simply does not let them have the foreign exchange
they would need for continental travel. At most, by traveling on British planes and ships, and by all sorts of subter-
fuges even the virtuous British will indulge in for the sake
of a continental holiday, a few manage to squeeze in a few
weeks in the sunshine. You will indeed see them in Paris, in
Switzerland, on the Riviera, in their accustomed haunts.
If you have taken seriously the rhetoric of American commentators who state with beautiful simplicity that the British can no longer travel at all in Europe, you will be surprised to see so many of them. Still, there is only a trickle
where there used to be a flood, and those continental Europeans who used to complain so bitterly about the demand-
ing British, always wanting tea, baths, and food without
decent sauces, are now complaining bitterly about their
absence.

Exchange restrictions do indeed weigh on most nationals of Western Europe, the lucky Swiss excepted. Some of the slack in the tourist industry has, however, been taken up by travel within one's own country. The English may not be able to go abroad, but they can—and do—flock to their own resorts. They still display their great national addiction to the seaside, but they spill over into the interior. Keswick in the Lake Country in summer would shock Wordsworth and Southey, and the peak of Helvellyn is thickly peopled the moment the clouds lift, which they occasionally do. The French travel a good deal in France, in spite of, or perhaps because of, inflation.

All in all, the traveler in Western Europe in mid-century, unless he is Mr. Shirer, will feel most of the time that he is in quite familiar, even normal, surroundings. No one, it must be repeated, can fail to see the traces of the last war. They are not pleasant to see. But neither are they omnipresent, and as we shall see, they are slowly being obliterated as the peoples of Western Europe rebuild. And, unwelcome though the reflection may be to sensitive idealists, it is a fact that Western man has long been in the habit of destroying in wars and revolutions the patient and often lovely works of peace. This last war, at least, was not apocalyptic; much, much more of the accumulated architectural work of generations of Western Europeans remains than has been destroyed. The next war may destroy Canterbury and Chartres, Beauvais (hard hit, but structurally still intact, a tribute to the soundness of medieval building even at its climax of obsession with sheer height) and everything else the Middle Ages have left us; but this war most emphatically did not.

The Material Basis

But these are mere scraps of a traveler's impressions. We must come back to the general, to statistics, if we are to have a sound scaffolding for a knowledge of the temper of Western Europe. As I have already noted, the complexity and scale of our problems make this kind of abstraction absolutely essential; it is only the abuse of these methods, the exclusive reliance on long chains of deductions from initial assumptions, that need worry us.

Now the inescapable thing about the economic state of contemporary Western Europe is this: both as a whole, and in each of its constituent national units, it is "richer" right now in the 1950's than ever before in history. Two world wars and a Great Depression have in fact left even that center of war, Western Europe, materially better off than before. This is a challenging statement, and I have put it baldly. I shall shortly seek to establish it as true, and explain it. It is, however, in itself neither a justification nor a palliation of war. I confess that I make it not without a certain emotional satisfaction at confronting the prophets of doom with a fact which I know will hardly shake their pessimism. But I do not make it gloatingly. It is not directed at the moralist, not even at the tender-minded, but only at those whose moral abhorrence of war takes the form of refusing to weigh at all the evidence in the case.

The basic explanation for the material reëstablishment of Europe—apart from whatever it is in human nature or social structure that keeps men at work—is of course that our technological and economic methods enable building to keep roughly in pace with destruction. We can destroy faster and on a bigger scale than ever before but we can build faster and on a bigger scale than ever before. There is a time lag—we do not build quite as fast as we destroy; but the general proposition holds. This balance between tearing down and building up, like the somewhat comparable balance in actual warfare between attack and defense, has clearly held true up to the present. It is, like all such balances in human affairs, a very rough one, often seriously disturbed, and of course a generalized, statistical balance of no consolation to the individual who faces absolute destruction, and of no indisputable moral value to the individual who faces absolute despair.

There are those who hold that modern technology—in particular, the atomic bomb—has ended this rough general balance between destruction and rebuilding; and some of them go on to the assertion that Western Europeans know this, know that the next war will be fought in their lands, and are haunted by this fear. Both the proposition that destruction is inevitable and the proposition that ordinary Europeans are haunted, obsessed, by the fear of destruction we must take to be unproven. The first proposition I am not competent to pronounce on, and fear indeed that it is the kind of proposition that cannot be tested save empirically. The second proposition I do not find consonant with my experience of Western Europe; at any rate, this haunting fear has not prevented the haunted from working hard, regularly, and effectively to rebuild their economies. Perhaps indeed they work out of sheer desperation, but again, I don't think so. Furthermore, good observers have reported that Europeans seem for the most part less completely haunted by fear of the next war than Americans—or at any rate, than American intellectuals.

Finally, we come to my original statement that the countries of Western Europe are "richer" now than at any other time. This vague term can be broken down into all sorts of terms for which there are statistical measures available—national income, gross national product, indices of industrial and agricultural production, and the like. I limit myself to three significant sets of indices. They come from the Statistical Office of the United Nations, which, granting the uncertainties and difficulties of this sort of statistics, seems to me about the best available source.

First, indices of mining and manufacturing production for all of Western Europe: from a base of 100 in 1937, production was still only 79 in 1947 and 92 in 1948; in 1949 the base of 1937 was exceeded with 105, in 1950 with 117, in 1951 with 128. Since the population index for Europe excluding the USSR was 107 in 1950, compared with 100 in 1936, it is clear that this rise in production means also a small rise in productivity per capita.

Second, a table taken from the *Statistical Yearbook* for 1952 (Statistical Office of the United Nations, New York, 1952, pp. 90–98) which gives index numbers for manufacturing industries by separate countries. The sources vary, and some of the indices are for "general" industrial production, including mining. But they are roughly comparable, and the interested reader can go back to the sources for technical details.

Third, indices of national income *in constant prices* by certain countries: France, 100 in 1938, 106 in 1949; Netherlands, 100 in 1938, 127 in 1951; Switzerland, 100 in 1938, 128 in 1950. The comparable figures for Great Britain unfortunately use 1946 for a base with 100; but even here the index had climbed to 113 in 1950. These are figures for total

Table 2.   Indices of Industrial Production
(1948 = 100)

	1937	*1952 (March)*
Austria	112	180
Denmark	78	118
France	96	133
West Germany	—	236
Ireland	78	125
Italy	102	144
Luxembourg	100	125
Netherlands	88	127
Norway	80	122
Spain	74 (1938)	133
Sweden	67	115
United Kingdom	88	126
United States	57	115

national income; but those for per capita income also show rises for these countries. All have been corrected for inflation.

Statistics are easily overdone, but here is a final set, one which puts my general argument for Western European prosperity, or at least normality, in the least favorable light. Here are estimates of the actual daily per capita food supplies in calories for certain countries: France, prewar, 2,830, in 1950–51, 2,700; Netherlands, prewar, 2,920, in 1950–51, 3,020; Switzerland, prewar, 3,110, in 1950–51, 3,300; Great Britain, prewar, 3,120, in 1950–51, 3,080; Belgium-Luxembourg, prewar, 2,820, in 1950–51, 2,910. Though France and Britain still showed in 1950–51 slight deficits as compared with prewar days, their citizens were clearly, on an average, getting enough to eat, and these deficits have almost certainly been overcome by 1953. Incidentally, and I suppose because the human stomach has definite limits, the statistics for the United States do not here show their usual skyrocketing tendency as compared to those for Europe.

In 1950–51 our figure was only 3,233 calories, less actually than the 3,300 for Switzerland and the 3,460 for the Republic of Ireland, which is apparently the best, or at any rate the most, fed country in the world.

Now like all statistics that deal in totals and in averages per capita, these may conceal serious concrete cases of deficiencies. Notably they may conceal the fact that the poorest ten or twenty per cent of a population is actually suffering from want. I do not think the most hostile critic of the British socialist (or better, mixed) economy really thinks that the British working classes are worse off than before the war; in fact, almost everyone agrees that they are better off. British food always has been a subject about which Frenchmen, and even Americans, like to be patronizing. But the British working classes are certainly eating better, medically speaking at any rate, than before the war. They are getting more milk and more vegetables, and somewhat more meat. Nor in general can one say that these classes in the smaller democracies are worse off. A good many vocal Frenchmen think that their own working classes are worse off, and this opinion is often echoed in the United States. I can only say that after traveling some five thousand miles through France in the fall and winter of 1952–53, I did not as a mere traveler notice what seemed to me serious and extensive deprivation. And I must add that the mere traveler, unless he is really ridden by preconceptions, cannot help noticing phenomena such as serious malnutrition in a population, especially among children, as anyone who saw German and Austrian cities immediately after the war of 1914–1918 can testify.

For a final concrete evidence that Western Europe is not wholly sunk in economic decay we need not go into statistics. Everyone who has been recently in Western Germany agrees that it is humming with industry, that apparently not even Allied bombings totally destroyed industry, that what rebuilding and retooling was necessary has in fact added to Germany's industrial efficiency. It would certainly be much better in every way if the dangers of obsolescence or economic old age could be decisively overcome by somewhat less cruel and stupid methods than warfare, but the fact seems to be that industrialists have a hard time bringing themselves to scrapping plant and machinery in peacetime. Mars is less conservative than boards of directors.

Eight years after the war, then, Western Europe has made up for the actual crude economic damage it suffered. This statement does not mean that everything destroyed has been replaced—far from it—nor does it amount to the statement that war is in effect a net economic stimulus. We should be better off morally and economically—indeed, we should be better off economically just because we should be better off morally—had the war not been a necessity. But for what these statistics measure, for the gross collective wealth of Western Europe, those prophets of doom who say that modern war has been absolutely destructive, has lessened the total wealth of nations, are clearly wrong.

In an interesting article, "Europe's Invisible Brick Wall," in *Harper's Magazine* for August 1953, Mr. Peter F. Drucker recognizes the "spectacular" economic recovery Western Europe made up to about 1951, a recovery reflected clearly in the figures I have just cited. But he points out, quite accurately indeed, that with the exception of West Germany, the corresponding figures for the last two years, incomplete though they are, show a definite flattening out of the curve of production. This flattening out alarms him. It shows, he maintains, that the Western Europeans have not really learned their economic lesson properly from us Americans. By prodigious efforts they have made up for their war losses, but they show no signs that they can gear their economy to the standards of Detroit and Texas. They are still essentially conservative, still at bottom unwilling to share a greatly increased production with their working classes. We shall in later chapters return to some phases of this problem. But right here we should note that, again with the possible exception of the Germans, most European businessmen and even government planners find it hard to forget that our American new-model perpetually dynamic economy came a fearful cropper in 1929. They are still not quite persuaded that it is safe to keep up a too "spectacular" rise in the indices of production. They may be wrong. But in itself their caution is by no means a sign of failure of nerve or energy, and in the long run it is probably just as well, if Europe is to be Americanized industrially, that the process should not be too violent and too rapid.

The destruction of human lives brings up even more acutely the moral problem. It is an evil thing for one man to be killed in war. Nevertheless, we must not even here neglect the facts. There are more people alive in Western Europe as a whole today than ever before. Statistics do not measure at all the individual tragedies of war. They are not even very accurate for total deaths and permanently disabled among the armed forces. They cannot begin to measure the broken lives among the families and the friends of the dead and disabled. The last war, if it did not kill men and women beyond the power of human reproductiveness to replace them, if even in this respect it was not as much worse than that of 1914–1918 as the most alarmist thinkers, like Mr. Sorokin, had predicted, was very bad indeed. The race was spared last time an epidemic like the influenza of 1918, which killed more than were killed in action. But the wholesale murders of Jews, the uprooting of whole populations, especially in Eastern Europe, and above all the fearful portent of Hiroshima, must give the most hard-boiled realist pause.

Yet *for the particular region with which we are here concerned*, the total loss of human life was not appreciably greater, and may have been rather less, than in 1914–1918. British Empire forces lost nearly a million in the first war, and some 350,000 in the second. French casualties were 1,385,000 killed in the first war. For the second, figures cannot be very clear because of the difficulties of estimating deaths in the resistance forces, but they were much less than a million. Casualties in the German armed forces were much worse this time than the 1,808,000 in 1914–1918, probably somewhere near 3,000,000. Even if one includes civilian deaths, chiefly from enemy air bombardment, the total number of human lives lost directly because of the war in Western Europe in 1939–1945 was not greatly in excess of five or six million. Casualties—killed, wounded, prisoners—in Eastern Europe and Asia and in the rest of the world may justify the estimates released by the United States War Department on July 24, 1945, for the whole war: 60,000,-000 in contrast with 37,000,000 in the war of 1914–1918. But it must be repeated: for *Western Europe* the blood-letting was no worse than last time, and for the United Kingdom and France, it was definitely less.

If we may use a little longer the heartless language of demographic statistics, it would appear that even the Ger-

mans, in 1953, are no less numerous than before the war—
a fact which the French do not cease to point out. The
great displacement of Germans in the East has made count-
ing heads difficult and uncertain. There were, however,
according to the last census of the Third Reich in 1939,
69,032,242 people in territories then under the German
flag. The best current estimates today for both Western
Germany and Eastern Germany—and excluding Austria—
are about the same, some 70,000,000.

Once more I must insist that I am not here trying to
make a comparison between the moral and spiritual in-
cidence of the last two great wars. However such a comparison is to be made, it is not to be made by the demog-
rapher and the statistician. There remains, indeed, a
concrete and in part material and therefore measurable kind
of war damage worth a word here, for again this damage,
great though it was in the last war, by no means equaled
what the alarmists still seem to feel it must have been. I
refer to the destruction of works of art. It has been great,
and the destruction of one minor parish church of Christopher Wren's would be too much. But the artistic heritage
of the past, seen as a whole, has suffered quantitatively
nothing like complete destruction. Priceless things have
been blown to bits, but more priceless things remain. A
rapid survey of the reports confirms what we have already
noted as a mere traveler's impression.

In the first place, the "phony war" in the West allowed
the authorities time to store in safety the greater part of
the most precious paintings and sculptures in private as well
as in public hands. Something was lost in the shuffle and the
Russians seem to have been in these matters as ruthless as
conquerors used to be in the past. But in the West at least

armies seem to have been amazingly conscientious about
the protection of works of art, far more so than were armies
as recently as the time of Napoleon. The masterpieces of
architecture cannot be moved for protection, and it is here
that the heritage of the Western past has suffered its greatest losses in this war. Of the half-dozen supremely great
French Gothic cathedrals none, however, was damaged as
badly as was that of Rheims in the war of 1914–1918. The
great Renaissance châteaux of the Loire were spared. In
England the stupid "Baedeker raids" of 1942 did surprisingly little damage and all the great medieval cathedrals are
basically unharmed. By great good luck the Germans at
Canterbury succeeded in damaging seriously only a very
frigid Victorian restoration of the library. Oxford was
never bombed, in spite of its great Morris motor works—
since, according to a widespread folk belief in England,
Hitler had designated Oxford as his capital for the occupation, and wished it to remain intact. Cambridge too survived
with no damage to its lovely colleges. The loss of many
Wren churches in the City of London is indeed deplorable,
but St. Paul's stood with no more than a hole in the North
Transept, quite reparable, and there are still many good
churches by Wren and his followers quite intact.

Nor was the damage in Italy as great as many of us feared
during the war it would be. Rome was spared, as were Ven-
ice and most of northern Italy. German destruction of the
approaches to the Arno bridges in Florence was a disaster,
but most of Florence is intact. Battle raged right through
the marvelously preserved Greek temple of Paestum in
southern Italy, which many think gives the best impression
of what a Greek temple was like of all now existing. Paestum is still there. In general, and in spite of the landings in

Sicily, the living record of the greatness of ancient Greece and Rome in Italy is as good as ever. Perhaps the most thoroughgoing destruction in Italy was that of the great historic monastery of Monte Cassino; but centuries of war and civil troubles, and even changes of taste, had already made Monte Cassino, however great its spiritual associations, a not very important monument of architecture.

In Germany certainly the loss for the lover of architecture was very great indeed. Berlin was a comparatively new city, and though there were no doubt those who loved it—though one must not be heartless in such matters—it was not on the whole a lovely city. But the loss of some of the most fascinating of medieval buildings, especially in Bavaria and in the heart of Frankfurt-am-Main, is irreparable, and worst of all, though since it is in the Russian zone Westerners cannot readily check the damage for themselves, is the apparent destruction of the greatest of baroque cities, Dresden. Still, once more, Germany has by no means been leveled to the ground. Much more even of the Middle Ages remains than has been destroyed, and the Germans, with their fondness for the Middle Ages and their great scholarly fund of knowledge of them, can be trusted to do a good job of restoration.

We must, however, return to the more mundane facts of contemporary European economic life. Now I do not wish to be understood as saying that all is serene on the economic front in Western Europe. The region as a whole, and its separate nation-states, are clearly not yet economically retrogressive in terms relative to their own past. Their rates of growth have indeed—as have, incidentally, such rates in New England—slowed down in comparison with some periods of the nineteenth or early twentieth centuries, but they still have dynamic economies. Their basic difficulties in a material sense stem from the fact that other parts of the world are growing faster industrially, making it more difficult for these Western European nations to sell outside their area the manufactured goods and the economic services which they have to exchange for food and raw materials to supply their dense populations. Though France at a pinch—a most unrealistic pinch that could never really come—could feed and clothe and house its millions at something near present standards wholly on the basis of internal trade, or national autarky, Western Europe as a whole has to export or give up its present standard of living. And one thing is very clear and must never be forgotten: contemporary West Europeans are used to a high standard of living, and are in no mood to accept a lower one.

Historically, Western Europe has been able to build itself up as the great center of material civilization because its particular skills in industry, shipping, finance, government, and war were greater than those of other peoples. The basic exchange—for it was an exchange, and no mere exploitation—was that of Western European finished goods and economic services for food and raw materials produced in other parts of the world. You may call those other parts of the world "colonial" if you like, and rub your hands with glee now that the colonies are getting their own back. I suspect that some centuries from now a conscientious and decently remote historian will be able to record this long process from Da Gama and Columbus to the present as on the whole the least purely exploitative, the most nearly a fair exchange, of all the prolonged contacts in the past between materially superior and materially inferior societies and civilizations. Europeans killed natives, and even snubbed them; yet somehow the natives got richer and more numerous.

But we need not draw the problem of the past of colonialism as a red herring across the trail of the problem we are engaged on. The point is that there are now in Western Europe millions of people—some fifty millions or more at a very rough guess—in excess of the number which could be maintained at their present standards of living were the area somehow sealed off from the rest of the world. But the area, in spite of the wilder prophets of doom, is certainly not now so sealed off. As I have tried hard to show, these extra men and women are still living, and not—again we speak in general terms, not in those of private lives of individuals—living in misery.

They are living as well as they are for a great number of reasons, some of which I propose to consider. Americans will perhaps think first of all, naturally enough, of the Marshall Plan and its successors. No one should minimize the importance of the aid we have brought to Europe. Indeed no one who remembers, say as an index to our former state of mind the remark attributed to Calvin Coolidge about the war debts of 1914–1918, "They hired the money, didn't they," should fail to recognize that we have, whatever our motives—and I think we can say with due understatement that they have been mixed—achieved an extraordinary change of mind and policy. But we must not exaggerate. We have not wholly supported a good-for-nothing indigent Europe. Our aid over the years has not been more than the "pump-priming" it was designed to be. It has been a marginal aid, aid which has made the crucial difference between struggling along and getting ahead.

More important quantitatively than American aid has been the fact that, again contrary to the prophets of doom, the basic relation between Western Europe and some at least of the rest of the world we can simply call the "colonial system" has not at one stroke been destroyed. Raw materials still come in to Liverpool and Marseille, Antwerp and Rotterdam, and finished goods and services still go out from them. This trade is in part still something like the old colonial trade; that is, it goes out from a mother country to a relatively undeveloped true colonial dependency, goes out from Britain, France, or Belgium to tropical Africa or to Malaya, to Madagascar or Belgian Congo. It is in part a newer development of such trade, between a European manufacturing and banking mother country to a free or partly free dependency still predominantly a supplier of raw materials. Such is the classic trade between Britain and her self-governing dominions—to which India, Ceylon, and Pakistan still belong—between France and French North Africa. It is in part trade between such European countries and "sovereign" states in various parts of the world which are still willing and able to trade their raw materials for finished goods. Trade between Britain and the Argentine, for instance, though it is not what it was in the Victorian heyday, is still a major factor in the British economy, as the recent hard-won trade agreement between the two countries should remind us.

Finally, some of this life-giving trade is of the kind that the more hopeful classical economists of the last century held would someday be the great form of international trade, exchange of their most advantageously produced commodities among fully matured balanced industrial economies. We American masters of all the material arts still do consume British jams and biscuits, British woolens, even British motorcars, French wines and other luxury goods, Swiss watches, German optical instruments and hardware, and a great deal else from all parts of Europe. We Americans still travel on foreign ships and planes, still use European financial services, and of course still spend much more as tourists there than Europeans do as tourists here. At the risk of being tedious, I must once more insist that not even the unheard-of, unprecedented revolutionary changes of our lifetime—I use the favorite language of our publicists—have totally changed the conditions of international trade. A Cobden brought back to life would certainly be deeply shocked by the world of the 1950's, but he would, if he kept his sanity, not find it wholly unrecognizable.

In short, bad as the world looks today, Western Europe can prosper economically if the world gets no worse. Europe is unlikely again to be the overwhelmingly major industrial and financial center of the world. She can, however, remain an important part of the world. But are there perhaps reasons internal to Western Europe, factors of weakness that threaten absolute instead of relative economic decline? We arrive at the most delicate point of our analysis of the economic basic of present-day Western Europe.

The central point the pessimists make is this: Generally speaking, and with exceptions here and there, especially for those marvelous people the Germans, who seem almost as gifted in technology and industrial organization as we Americans, Western Europeans cannot produce efficiently enough to compete successfully in any kind of world market we are likely to have. Their PMH—production per man hour—simply isn't high enough to compete with "younger" peoples, ourselves, the Canadians, the Japanese, perhaps even the Russians. The analysts give varied sets of reasons for this European lack of efficiency. The favorite one in American conservative circles is a simple blanket explanation: Western Europe has gone or is going socialist, with the greatest and richest nation, Great Britain, in the lead. And of course no socialist country, say the conservatives, can compete with a country where private ownership, rugged individualism, and laissez faire still prevail. Another explanation dwells on the age of European plant and organization. Europe led the world industrially, and precisely because of this fact she is now suffering from the handicaps of economic old age, obsolescent equipment, exhausted natural resources—here the British coal industry is held up as a horrid example of the multiple ills of old age—and, a rather more subtle point, a lack of willingness to experiment with new techniques and products, a drying-up of inventiveness and entrepreneurial daring, a blocking of the career open to talent, in short, psychological old age, if not senility, among the managers.

Another variant argument stresses the inability or unwillingness of the West European laboring classes to work hard and effectively; they are said to be corrupted by a socialist desire to get something for nothing, by an old-fashioned laboring-class solidarity which makes them resent a fellow worker who tries to earn more than the average, by a mistaken feeling that their employer is their natural enemy. This last is a feeling which some critics say is justified enough, since their employers have not seen

the light, as American employers have, and have refused to
give them the higher share of their product they need if
mass industry is to work. Other economic analysts extend
this kind of blame to all social classes in Europe, maintaining that industrialists, farmers, and workers are all
intent on too high standards of personal consumption, that
they refuse to accept that abstention from immediate consumer's goods without which not enough of the gross
national product is plowed back into means of increased
production, that is, capital investment. The broadest and
most hopeless analysis of all adds as a final damning factor
the assertion that the little peninsula we call Europe, although it had the coal, iron, climate, and other basic resources to give it the lead in the first industrial revolution,
now lacks the oil, hydroelectric potential, nonferrous
metals, even the sheer market area, needed to enable it to
keep up with the second industrial revolution of our own
time.

All this adds up to a gloomy analysis indeed, and it is
tempting to agree with the economic experts both here
and abroad who have come to the sad conclusion that the
best that can be done for poor senile Europe is to devise the
kind of considerate treatment of the patient they call "economic geriatrics." But I do not think the picture is as black
as they paint it, and I propose to take up very briefly the
pessimistic arguments I have just brought forward. But do
not misunderstand me. I am not trying to make a mechanical
rebuttal of these arguments, and come out with the conclusion that all is well in contemporary Europe. There is
some truth in all these arguments, and I am trying to do
no more than estimate the degree of truth they have.

The least sound I believe is the ecological argument that

Europe has not got the resources to maintain a reasonable degree of prosperity in our neo-technical age. It is true that there is almost no oil in Western Europe, and that many of the regions with a great economic past, notably Britain, Benelux, and Germany, haven't the kind of rivers that can be harnessed to provide great hydroelectrical power. But the one safe generalization about technology is that it is always changing, and that it is quite impossible to predict its future. It looks to a layman as if we were on the verge of a third industrial revolution, in which the key factor will be, not coal nor oil nor water power, but sun power or perhaps atomic power. Unless indeed we cannot get beyond the very scarce uranium, which seems unlikely, it would seem that Europe starts with as high a potential in atomic power—apart from human factors of industrial and political organization—as the rest of the world. If we are to run on sun power, the future looks gloomy for the British Isles; but even there the sun shines more than American folklore will let it. It is indeed true that Western Europe is at present too politically subdivided to provide the large free market area that the most efficient modern industrial organization requires; but to this problem of breaking down present political and economic barriers in Europe we must return later in this study.

In itself, the reproach of "socialism" seems to me almost pointless. All Western nations, including the United States, are in 1953 so far from the theory, and even the practice, of classical economics, the economics of the Manchester School, that the conscientious present-day follower of the school—there are a few left, for principles die hard—must feel that all nations are almost equally far from the right way. It would be interesting but most unscientific to try to rank Western countries along a simple numerical scale like a thermometer, between a freezing point marked "socialism" and a boiling point marked "capitalism." One would need for each country a number of criteria, extent of actual nationalization of industry, actual recruitment and reward of managers, size and efficiency of industries, degree of monopoly or oligopoly in various industries, degree of government regulation, and many more. I strongly suspect that the United States would by no means come out close to the capitalism of the classical economists. On a simple centigrade scale from the zero of socialism to the 100 of capitalism, I hazard the crude guess for the United States of 60, for Britain of 40, with France at 70 and Western Germany somewhere in between the United States and Britain.

This is of course very crude guessing indeed, and I am probably basing my guess rather strongly, not so much on criteria of public or private ownership, as on the contrast between real individual ownership and managership on the capitalist side and impersonal ownership separated from bureaucratic management on the socialist side. Let me be concrete once more. I have recently been involved in a relation, perhaps even a quarrel, with an enormous department store, a relation which started with a mere misspelling of my name on their accounts. Before I got through, all the smear words of the capitalist attack on socialism—red tape, bureaucracy, irresponsibility, impersonal hugeness, general snafu—rose to my mind, and were not always successfully suppressed. I suggest that it is not by ideas about private initiative and government ownership that differences in modern economic organization of states are to be measured, but in the actual structure and practice of

economic life. If this is so, the X and Co. with whom I
quarreled is much more comparable with a government
bureau here or in Europe than with the X and Co. of the
old merchant prince who founded it in the nineteenth
century. The difference between the store of the merchant
prince and the store today is by no means wholly one of
size, though size is certainly important; it is also a difference
in the spirit and methods of management, in the way the
whole staff is trained and held together. It's as good a store
as it ever was, but of course it's not as efficient as it used
to be, in part because they are trying so damned hard to
be efficient.

This brings me to what I consider the really important
element in the pessimistic analyses of European economic
conditions I have been trying to correct. This is the assertion that the West Europeans can't keep a dynamic
economy going because they haven't the right spirit, the
right temper, to work hard enough, the assertion that they
prefer butter not only to guns, but to machine tools. With
the technical economic argument that Western Europe as
a whole consumes too much and invests too little I am not
enough of a specialist to deal competently. I do, however,
note that the economic doctors disagree on this matter,
both as to diagnosis and as to remedy, and I incline to the
belief that the patient will survive. For Europeans, whether
from climate, schooling, religion, economic necessity, or
just plain habit, have been good sound disciplined workers
for centuries, and *as a group* couldn't possibly stop for long
being such workers, even if a cosmic Santa Claus suddenly
brought them all they needed to live on. Impatient American travelers sometimes notice British workingmen knocking off for tea—and indeed at any hour of the day it would

be hard not to find someone in Britain knocking off and brewing tea. But these Americans have apparently never noticed American workingmen, following the advertisements as like good Americans they should, pausing for the pause that refreshes. Of course the automatic coke machine over in the corner by the rest room is neater and more efficient than any way of making tea—that water for tea just has to be boiling. But I must say I was much impressed with the polished chromium tea wagon they rolled in for elevenses in a great Piccadilly motor firm. The young lady who rolled it in looked like Miss Piccadilly 1952.

There is indeed a difference in tempo in the way we work and the way West Europeans work, but it is not an enormous, not a fundamental difference. The really central thing is the relation between workers—including farmers— and employing and government classes. If it is true that French workers hate their employers, if it is true that British workers want complete nationalization, if it is true even generally and more vaguely that European workers feel put upon by their bosses, then prospects will be bad until these conditions improve. For you cannot run a modern economy effectively very long if the class struggle is a clear, simple, and intense conflict between workers and employers. I do not think conditions in France, let alone in the rest of Western Europe, are as bad as that. But I do think that we could help Europe most if we could somehow export to them, not just goods or even industrial technology, but some of the art of softening the class struggle, of satisfying the human side of industry, which to the indignation, indeed frank disbelief, of the old-fashioned American liberal we really seem to have developed in this country. Meanwhile, there is one hopeful concrete index

which may indicate no more than that Europe is in some
kind of a boom period, no mean thing in itself, not in itself
a cause for tears: almost everywhere the number of production hours lost in strikes is less, often a great deal less,
than before the last war.

As I write, in mid-August of 1953, France, in any reck-
oning one of the key countries of Western Europe, is
indeed in the midst of a very serious wave of strikes,
political rather than purely economic in purpose. They
were set off by Premier Laniel's attempt to arrest inflation
by reducing wages. They were greeted in the American
press by the usual chorus of disapproval which we nowadays voice so freely in commentary on the efforts of our
partners of 1778 to work out a viable democracy. We
should, of course, be a bit more tactful and considerate, if
only because we ourselves seem not yet to have been en-
tirely successful in our efforts to stop our own milder but
very real inflation by the opposite process of increasing
wages. To the historian, M. Laniel's problem, and his
basically conservative solution, are strongly reminiscent
of Poincaré's at least temporarily successful effort to save
the franc in the mid-twenties. There is indeed no guarantee
that he will be even as successful as was his predecessor.
Indo-China is a worse running sore than was the occupation of the Ruhr. The French middle classes are weaker
than they were in the mid-twenties, the French working
classes more angry, perhaps more revolutionary. At this
writing it would take a very rash prophet indeed to assert
that the crisis will end with a stable France and a stable
franc. Yet the basic economic position of France is a sound
one. The country is not, like Britain, Benelux, and West
Germany, so completely industrialized as to be almost

wholly at the mercy of export trade. The French have an economy well balanced between industry and agriculture, at bottom a modest economy, based on relatively small enterprises, that cannot give them anything like world-leadership, but that can give them the material basis for a flourishing civilization. They may indeed be on the point of throwing all this away in a series of disastrous class struggles with no one the victor. But once more the historian will be cautious, for he knows the history of France is full of crises which might have, but did not, destroy state and society. The modern French in particular have for many generations refused to behave in politics the way their Anglo-Saxon critics on both sides of the Atlantic have thought—and announced firmly and freely—they ought to behave. They have not, at least since 1789, been decent, quiet, and stable, like the British; *their* strikers do not play soccer with the police, as it is said the British strikers did in the general strike of 1926. It is true that French strikes are not quite as bloody as ours used, until quite recently, to be. But this fact simply points up the more fundamental fact that nations come even further than do individuals from seeing themselves as others see them. The French have been almost as violent and quarrelsome in politics as we Americans—but they have not had a fine empty continent to quarrel in. Even so, they have hitherto stopped short of self-destruction. They have made the necessary compromises, and the safest bet is that they will do so again.

To sum up: Western Europe today, despite the destruction caused by the two wars of our time, has more people and a greater total wealth than at any time in the past. It faces grave problems indeed, problems in part economic.

But they are even more problems of the kind I have tried to suggest in my title for this book, "The Temper of Western Europe." They are problems involving the whole nature of man, *homo sapiens*—and perhaps his ambivalent other self, *homo stultus*—but certainly not of that quite imaginary creature, *homo oeconomicus*, in whom the economists themselves seem to have given up belief nowadays. To some of the abiding factors in these problems, to the persistent past, we must now turn.

III

The Persistent Past

Rebuilding

In spite of the horrors of the last thirty years, the total material wealth of Western Europe is, as I have pointed out in the last chapter, greater now than ever before. Much of that wealth is a heritage of the past. I turn to the past here, not for its own sake, but because so much of the past is inevitably the present. The interplay in human affairs between past and present to make the future, between habit and invention to push us along in changing but never unprecedented ways, comes out nicely in the problems of reconstruction of the war-torn cities of Europe. In London the lovers of the past would restore every little lane in that fearfully devastated region around St. Paul's, put back every Christopher Wren church, whether or not it had any parishioners; the planners, the lovers of the future, however, would actually pull down a few buildings spared by the bombs, and have a fine uninterrupted green park going right down to the Thames. Already the extremists on both sides have lost, but I think it pretty clear that the British "middle of the way" will turn out to be pretty far over toward the side of tradition, as usual. We shall have Paternoster Row again.

The city of Tours in France seems to me an even better

illustration of the point I am trying to make, for its restoration balances past and future neatly, with French *mesure*. There was not much *mesure* in its destruction. The center of the city was bombed and burned out by the Germans, along with so many of the crossings of the Loire, in those terrible June days of 1940 when the French army was still in being—and in retreat. Allied bombing in 1944 added to the destruction. Rebuilding has been going on steadily since the end of the war. They are not restoring the maze of streets of the old city, though they are restoring the churches and one fine Renaissance house. They are building pleasant squares and moderately wide streets, though still not quite wide enough for perfect car parking in the days to come. They are building according to plan in an inoffensive if undistinguished style which looks roughly like later French eighteenth-century building stripped of most of its ornamentation.

The influence of the past, and the tough persistence with which the human race goes on giving the lie to the prophets of doom, comes out especially in the treatment of the bombed-out shopkeepers of Tours. Anyone even mildly addicted to planning anywhere in the West would be delighted to diminish the number of retail shops, which are wastefully numerous and inefficient. The new Tours surely could get along with fewer tobacconists, fewer cafés, fewer newsdealers and booksellers, fewer equivalents of our American gift shoppes. But clearly it won't. Every little bombed-out shopkeeper felt he had a right to keep on, and the government at once began building temporary wooden huts along the wide boulevards spared destruction. There you still find the shops, the crowds as lively as ever about them, doing business in the old determined, inefficient way.

As the new buildings are finished, in go the shopkeepers on the ground floor, christening the bright new quarters with flowers and champagne, and one more set of temporary wooden buildings can be torn down. The new Tours will, I suspect, have substantially the same ratio of retail shops to inhabitants as the old—perhaps indeed a slightly larger one, since the motorcar in France is doing what it has done here, in the United States, weakening the smaller local centers of retailing and building up the larger ones.

Nationalism

Certain elements in European life persist, like the shopkeepers of Tours, in spite of the blows of fate and the promises of the planners. The first of these is national patriotism. For a long time now the term "nationalism" has had generally unfavorable connotations among intellectuals and the intellectual classes in the West. Even in France, where Charles Maurras may stand as the pure intellectual reduced to the absurd, his "integral nationalism" never commanded the allegiance of more than a minority of the French intellectual classes. We find it hard to realize that once, in the days of Mazzini and his peers, national patriotism was on the side of the angels, on the side of progress, liberalism, democracy. Most of us do indeed know that Marx has been proved wrong in thinking that the working classes of the West would soon be tied together with a cosmopolitan class-consciousness far stronger than their feeling toward the political state to which they belonged. But we still have as a kind of hangover from Marxism and other forms of rationalism a belief that somehow nationalism got invented about 1789 and has been foisted as a kind of opium of the people on human beings who might otherwise now all be happy citizens of the world. To many of my friends in the movement for some kind of world government, nationalism seems a fake, an illusion, an argument brought up by misguided people like me, but nothing that can't be destroyed, or at least tamed into something merely cultural, with a few strokes of the pen when the right people sign the Constitution of the World. Nationalism, at least in the sense of traditional insistence on political independence or sovereignty of the political unit, they say, makes no sense in our modern world of atomic bombs and large-scale production. A sovereign France does not make sense: therefore there really is no sovereign France.

I am of course caricaturing their position, but caricature is, one hopes, one of the possible roads to truth. The thoughts and feelings of millions of men and women, which we sum up so coldly and abstractly as nationalism, are the facts—the clinical material, if the figure of speech does not offend you too much—which we ought to try to understand before we deal with them on too large a scale and too radically. Let us take France, since to use France as an example of nationalism seems to come natural to Americans. We might indeed take the United States as an example, but there are probably good psychological reasons why we don't. A great deal of the past, before 1789 as well as after it, has gone into making most Frenchmen proud of being French, sharing in the "pooled self-esteem" of the living and the dead, and not taking orders from non-Frenchmen. As Professor Hayes has shown, France is a "nation of patriots" in part because educators, lawmakers, publicists, pressure groups of all kinds have worked so hard and so long to make it so. But the point is that such work cannot be undone at all quickly. Indeed, in the study of human affairs the familiar opposition of nature and environment is for pressing current problems altogether meaningless. It does not at all matter whether French nationalism grew spontaneously or was deliberately implanted by a scheming few. It is there, now, to be reckoned with.

Perhaps we Americans in particular underestimate the strength of nationalism in other peoples because, like the French of the great Revolution and Napoleon, our own nationalism is so firmly universalist, so almost innocently missionary in spirit. We feel sure that the rest of the world really would like to be Americans. We cannot easily understand, without a great effort at detachment and sympathy, that whole side of nationalism which stems from being, or having been, underdog, a status which at one time or other in the last five hundred years most European nations have suffered in. Southerners in this country should be able to understand that defeat makes the heart grow fonder, but among the many astonishing things about America is the fact that we do seem to have followed the "road to reunion" right to the end. A distinguished Spanish scholar, who knows his separatist Basques and Catalonians at home, is said to have had great difficulty in understanding why the Confederacy never tried it again. "Why," he said, "in my country they keep right on trying every generation or so."

I do not wish to be understood as maintaining that nationalism remains unchanged as a kind of ruling passion in the Western European countries. There are forces—but I lapse in jargon, there are real live human beings—working to transcend nationalism there. To them I shall return in a final chapter. But these people are working against others who have not yet gone far enough beyond nationalism. There are strong groups, such as the Gaullists in France and the reviving nationalist groups in Germany, for whom the nation *must* be sovereign. In Britain there are not only corresponding groups, essentially Tory in outlook, who wish to preserve the old sovereignty, but there are also many in the Labour party who feel that if Britain must somehow be integrated into a wider political community, that community must be found in closer ties within the Commonwealth or even with the United States, rather than with Western Europe.

It is almost certainly true that the old aggressive nationalism, that of Barrès, of Kipling, of *Deutschland ueber Alles*, is a much diminished faith, held only by unreconstructed fractions of the population, and even in Germany not worth the alarm they arouse in some of our American commentators. Nationalism among the many is perhaps no more than a kind of hangover, a habit, visible as a kind of distrust of foreigners, a normal parochialism of outlook. I know that many American travelers return from Europe with the feeling that, especially in France but also in Italy and in England, there is an active hatred of the United States, a kind of Americanophobia. Such travelers I think are unduly impressed with the profusion of inscriptions like "Americans, go home" and "Ridgeway la peste" which they see all over France, which are the work of an organized Communist minority in a country where Communists are still free to indulge in that kind of propaganda. Their opponents, who are I think stronger, are free to counter with inscriptions like "les Stalinistes à Moscou." Certainly many

European intellectuals are hostile to us, and it is the intellectuals who are most articulate. I do not think active hatred for the United States goes very far in the general population, not even in France. For what subjective impressions are worth I can only report that I did not feel this hostility toward myself as an American in 1952 any more than I had in the 1920's—not at least among the ordinary people a traveler meets.

It is sometimes held that nationalism is less strong, less of an obstacle to political integration, in the smaller than in the larger nations. This is true only in the very restricted sense that small countries like Belgium or Switzerland cannot possibly play the role of aggressor that Spain, France, Germany, and certainly overseas, Great Britain, have played at various times in modern history. But almost everyone who has worked for any kind of political or economic integration in contemporary Europe will tell you that the Swiss are about the hardest nuts to crack. It is not that the Swiss are wholly uncoöperative; they are up to a point good internationalists, as their history has made them. But they have stopped at about 1900. They seem to have made a fetish of their neutrality, and their feeling that this neutrality must be guarded at all costs has been, not unnaturally, strengthened by a guilty conscience. Their admirable democracy has twice within a lifespan done no fighting in defense of threatened democracy. They are not sure they can ride out a third storm, but they cannot—and for this I am sure we should not blame them—quite bring themselves to give up the old ways of neutrality that have carried them safely through two great storms. Even in the Low Countries, the efforts to bring Holland, Belgium, and Luxembourg together in "Benelux" have run

up against serious obstacles. Irish nationalism is not now
at the fever heat of 1921. Only a handful of Irish extremists
would still like to sink under the waters of the North
Sea the main island of Britain. But the Irish are always
touchy. They could not quite take the recent Coronation
in the fine spirit of vicarious enjoyment serenely republican
America took it, but had to pretend the Coronation was
none of their business. Irish nationalism still runs pretty
high, and seems unlikely to abate to a level that will bring
the Irish Republic to give up "sovereignty" until the
problem of Ulster is somehow solved.

Political Forms

The past, certainly the immediate past of half-a-dozen
generations, persists most conspicuously in political forms.
In the broadest possible area Western Europe can be made
to cover, that of all Europe outside the Iron Curtain, the
nineteenth century had introduced and in part acclimatized
some form of parliamentary democracy. Perhaps, since
democracy is so complex a cluster of ideas, we may content
ourselves with a rather simpler cluster, and say that Europeans by 1914 were used to the practice of *government by
discussion*—discussion in the open, with individual risks in
the support of radical stands greater in some countries than
others, but well short of the risks of totalitarian suppres-
sion. In Spain and Portugal, though I do not think conditions come near those of the late George Orwell's *1984*,
it is certainly stretching the point to say that there is nowadays true government by discussion. But everywhere else
in Western Europe the old ways of talking and writing it
out in public have survived two generations of prophets

who kept insisting we must all agree, and what is more important, some very thorough attempts to enforce one-party unity and all that goes with it.

If widespread public acceptance of the fact that human beings have different opinions and tastes—even, indeed above all, on very lofty matters—is as I believe one of the most important elements in democracy, then it is a fact that democracy is still firmly rooted in the area with which we are here concerned. The basic fact is accepted multani-mity, diversity of opinion on high matters. That mul-tanimity in the English-speaking countries is accommodated somehow in two or three national political parties; else-where in the free world it may need a dozen or more, with splinter parties constantly breaking off from them. It is a difficult question how far the two-party system may be considered the normal healthy form of democratic national government and how far the multiparty system may be considered a pathological condition. With very few inter-ludes, France has been in this latter condition for about one hundred and sixty-four years, which seems a long time for a really diseased organism to last.

The newspapers keep bringing us reminders that par-liamentary government on the continent is not what it is among us happy heirs of Magna Carta. French govern-ments fall like ninepins, and each time the pin boys seem to have a harder time setting them up again. De Gasperi is out in Italy, and Adenauer is not safe in Germany. Here again we cannot in a study of this scope attempt to go deeply into a problem that needs the most careful and considerate attention from Americans. It is a very serious problem indeed, and one which I have perhaps permitted myself undue levity about in my last few phrases. Yet it

must be insisted that the approach of many of our American
commentators on continental political forms is of a piece
with their general attitude of gloom and horror at the
failure of the universe to go the way Mr. Jefferson apparently hoped it would. Continental European democratic governments, like ours and those of the British
Commonwealth of Nations, get along from day to day
by a most complex balancing among the demands of all
sorts of competing interest-groups. It is an undue over-
simplification, but not a fundamental error, not a mis-
leading generalization, to put the matter this way: the
Europeans balance their group interests through the
mechanism of the multiparty system, and we and the
British balance ours through the mechanism of two parties
each of which is a congeries of diverse interests. (This is
especially true of the United States.) The compromises are
made at different points in the working of the two systems,
but the compromises are there in both. We make ours in
preëlection conventions, caucuses, and above all in the push
and pull of legislative committees and in the famous
negotiations between the White House and Capitol Hill.
These negotiations, by the way, seem sometimes to go
almost as badly, to exhibit almost as much unwillingness
to make decent compromises, as do the negotiations among
continental parties during a ministerial crisis. The Europeans, and most conspicuously the French, make their
compromises in the white light of such ministerial crises.

After all, it is hard not to grant Pope's famous couplet:

> *For forms of government let fools contest;*
> *Whate'er is best administer'd is best*

at least the status of a half-truth. Perhaps our system is, if
judged by the standards of political science, a better system

than the European. One can go too far in relativism in this as in other matters. Yet we Americans are still such good children of one phase of the eighteenth-century Enlightenment that we tend to the quite opposite error of assuming that there is a technically best engineered model in politics as in, say, the airplane, and that this model ought to work just as well in one country as in another. The important point is inescapable: in a democracy issues among interest-groups must be threshed out in public, and they must somehow be reconciled in political action. If they cannot be reconciled, no political machinery will make reconciliation possible, as we ourselves found out in 1861. The French machinery of government did survive the very great crisis of the Dreyfus Case early in this century. If the French really want to make their democracy work, they can do so even with the imperfect machinery of the Fourth Republic. We are back, as we have been before, at the root question of the temper of a people. If the French, and other Western Europeans, really are divided, something as we were in 1861, into two great groups essentially in a state of civil war, there will have to be a civil war, or at any rate a seizure of power by some group using non-democratic methods. But it is the thesis of this book that not even France, not even Italy, is at the moment so divided. But it is surely touch-and-go. Any very great shock to the still precarious material basis of West European life may well see an eclipse of democracy in one or more countries. But the fault will lie deeper than mere political machinery. The existing machinery, with all its faults, has proved in the past that it can provide a framework for the necessary, the grave and difficult compromises, on which democracy depends.

What I have been emphasizing in this discussion of Western European internal political structure is the persistence of that structure in the separate countries. This persistence is of importance, first because it seems to me a persistence of ways of living essentially democratic and second because it seems to me to make crystal clear that any future European political union will have to allow for a very great amount of national autonomy. These separate parties are all so rooted in their own countries that it seems impossible to merge them at first into what might be called European parties. This I believe to be true even where as with Catholic or old-fashioned socialist parties there is an apparent solid basis in ideas for getting beyond national political habits.

The fact of this political persistence hardly needs establishing here. Even where, as in West Germany and in Italy, we have witnessed something like a "restoration," a restoration which like the well-known Bourbon restoration in 1814 was in part at least imposed from the outside by victorious enemies—even in these once-fascist countries I am struck by the survival of old political ways. To the extent that these countries even before that great divide, 1914, were but marginally democratic, I think they remain marginally democratic. If you share the habits of thought of most American intellectuals, this statement will mean to you that those horrid Nazis and Fascists have been stupidly or wickedly allowed by somebody in responsible position to survive and revive, and that now it is too late. If you can approximate in these matters the relative detachment of the scientist, you will simply recognize that in human relations there is a complex set of phenomena most incompletely understood but which tend toward persistence, which have a kind of inertia. You will then recognize that in Germany and in Italy there are democratic survivals as well as totalitarian survivals, and that the fight still goes on.

But in France you find the neatest confirmation of the fact that in the ways of politics that tired, cynical but somehow not altogether discouraging folk-paradox holds true: *plus ça change plus c'est la même chose.* Nothing is quite so much like the Third French Republic as the Fourth. Party organization, party leadership, party journalism, even the details of parliamentary procedure are today substantially what they were twenty years ago. A lot of earnest and very able people tried hard after the Liberation of 1944 to mold France anew, and the fact that they encouraged the use of the locution "Fourth Republic" is a measure of their failure to effect real economic and spiritual changes. But again, we are not for the moment evaluating, nor even attempting to explain, but simply noting this persistence of the past. And here the persistence confronts with unusually simple irony the really grandiose claims to innovation made by the change from Third to Fourth. Indeed, I should think that almost any reflective person, political scientist or not, would come after reasonable study of the facts involved to the conclusion that the New Deal and the Fair Deal have changed the American Republic between 1932 and 1952 more fundamentally than the French Republic has been changed in those same years. Just to be provocative, I suggest that if we had the French habit of numerotation in these matters we should now be in the Fifth American Republic, the "revolutions" having come under Jefferson, Jackson, Lincoln, and Franklin Roosevelt.

At any rate, the past persists in European politics, and conditions the present. It is precisely on these bits of political machinery that the sentiments as well as the interests of men fasten, and by so fastening keep them working, even though they work poorly, even though blueprints for much better machinery are at hand. Nor is it just the selfish vested interests of the few who hold place, who run the machinery, which accounts for this persistence. Let me take an American instance familiar to all, and one in which no in-group feeling at all comparable to nationalism in intensity accounts for persistence. Our minor civil subdivisions, counties in most of the country, towns in New England, are affronts to reason and efficiency. I bring up the phrase "horse-and-buggy" and leave it at that.

Now the easy explanation of why we keep horse-and-buggy counties in these days of jet planes is that the officeholders want to keep them for purely selfish reasons. No doubt the vested interests of the officeholders is a factor, but surely not even in Georgia, where the counties are so numerous, nor in rural New England, where the towns are so numerous, are local officeholders a majority of the population. If the people of Georgia or of Vermont very much wanted fewer and more efficient local government areas they could get them. Perhaps it is mere inertia that prevents reform. But when you fall into that almost automatic "mere" you are gravely underestimating a very important thing. Real reform is of course possible, and in the field I am using for illustration it is being achieved. In a field the American people really do feel strongly about, education, we have already gone far to eliminate in favor of the central rural school a horse-and-buggy institution, the little red schoolhouse, which had behind it some strong emotions other than those I have summed up as inertia. I shall try to show later that this apparently local instance is not without bearing on the much wider problem of European unity.

The Persistent Social Structure

We are perhaps more prepared to accept the persistence of the past in social rather than in political structures. Yet even in this field a lot of Americans, and even Englishmen, seemed to believe that in 1945 the British "revolution by consent" was about to bring complete social equality to England, about to eliminate the distinction between gentlemen and others. I need hardly insist that there are still gentlemen in England. Most certainly there has been throughout Western Europe for several centuries a process summarily to be described as leveling, a squeezing together of the social pyramid—better, the socio-economic pyramid —both from top and bottom. This process has been very much hastened in the last two or three generations, but a pyramid remains, and not the nice straight line which one might take as the graphic representation of the ideal of the classless society.

Status is in our Western society a very subtle thing, and one which varies so much among the constituent states of this society, and indeed within each state, that only the partly intuitive understanding of the native, the member of the state, can grasp it. European visitors to the United States see readily enough that ours is indeed a stratified society, but they very often make the mistake of thinking that the principle of stratification is wholly economic, that in America a man is measured wholly by his wealth; and they compound their error by assuming the untrammeled operation of the career open to talents. Some Americans appear to make the same mistake, in spite of Middletown, Yankee City, and a host of other places our anthropologists and sociologists have shown to be by no means societies stratified by income alone.

Like so many of the topics we have had to touch upon here, this one of social status in Western society is far too big to receive proper treatment in a brief survey. I think I can best make the point I wish to make, that of the persistence of the past, if I limit myself to the two countries I know best, two countries which if they by no means exhaust the variety of Western European social structure, are at any rate quite typical. But I do not wish to claim exemption from the limitation I have just set up. I am neither an Englishman nor a Frenchman, and I have by no means the intuitive knowledge of their societies a native would have. Mine is an outsider's view.

Victorian England, a society for which Bagehot found the searching epithet "deferential," is indeed—I was about to fall into the easy stereotype and write "dead," but of course the metaphor is a bad one. Let us say that contemporary Elizabethan England is in many ways very different from Victorian England. I find a neat concrete illustration of the change in a great English estate now freely open to the public. The park is perhaps a little less meticulously gardened than in the time of the present earl's grandfather, but the castle, the lawns, and the oaks are still there, and still splendidly Victorian. Only, the castle has been divided up into apartments for workers in a nearby city, who go in by bus. The medieval courtyard is full of modern children, bicycles, and the whole apparatus of family life. His lordship, when he is not in London, lives in what used to be the gatekeeper's lodge.

The statistics confirm the isolated instance. The almost incredible income taxes—ninety-five cents on the dollar at the top levels—and the death duties have destroyed the economic basis of these great estates. I have throughout this study sought to emphasize, as against the exaggerations of the alarmists, the fact that in human affairs change is never as complete as it appears to these alarmists to be. But of course change is real. Indeed, one conspicuous change between, say, 1850 and 1950 is that in 1850 it was the optimists, not the pessimists, who held the floor with their exaggerations. But we are concerned here with the present. One specific piece of statistics is most eloquent. Just before the last war some 7,000 individuals in Great Britain had a net income after taxation of £6,000 or over, already a very great relative lopping off of the top of the economic pyramid as compared with Victorian times. But after nine short years, in 1946, those 7,000 individuals had been reduced to 45. And meantime the pound had somewhat depreciated in value.

If the great fortunes and the great estates are gone in Great Britain, there are abundant signs of the continued existence in something short of dire straits of a prosperous upper class or gentry. Many of them will complain bitterly about the servant problem, about taxes, about currency restrictions which keep them from continental travel. But Mayfair is peopled by them, supported by them; and between Mayfair and Islington or Poplar the social distance still greatly exceeds the geographic. There are those who hold that the British upper and upper middle classes are for the most part living off capital, and that their disappearance has merely been delayed. No doubt many individuals in this class are living off capital, but I think it is clear that the "mixed" economy of Britain provides still an adequate base in executive and professional salaries, in business profits, in return on capital—remember that none of the nationalized industries was confiscated, and that the old owners are still being paid off—to support these people, if not in the style to which they were accustomed, at least in a style that will for some time mark them off as a privileged class.

One can make a long list of British ways that have not vanished in this world quite as fast as they should have vanished had the revolution of 1945 measured up to what was then written and said about it. In the cathedral close at Wells or Salisbury you can believe that Bishop Proudie is still alive; and you know quite well that Mrs. Proudie is. Nor is this survival an illusion. I am quite aware of the traps prose fiction has for the historian and sociologist. The historian of A.D 3000 who concludes from our twentieth-century American "Westerns" in fiction and in movies that the West of 1950 is still the West of 1850 will make a mistake—but, by the way, not nearly as great a mistake as our own contemporaries who believe that East, West, North, and South have now been merged in one great uniform lump. Trollope's Barsetshire, I conclude quite without irony, is still on the map.

Perhaps the public school, which sometimes seems to Americans to belong to the same level of being as Barsetshire, will serve better as an example. Many of my British friends in wartime were quite sure that whatever else survived the Labour party victory they were sure was coming, the public school would have to go. Or if the grounds and buildings were too valuable to turn over to other uses, at least the school itself would be changed be-

yond recognition, opened to all classes, cleansed of snob-
bery, modernized in curriculum. That program still exists
on paper and in the minds of the New Fabians, but I do
not think anyone will seriously maintain that much has been
done to achieve it. I should guess that of all the Victorians,
the great schoolmasters brought magically back to life
today would find the little world of their profession most
unchanged. Certainly Arnold would feel more at home in
Rugby than Cobden in Manchester or Carlyle in Chelsea.

These are, however, details. The public school does bring
up the central general problem: are there signs that the
temper, the goals, the methods of the ruling class in Britain
are changing? This problem is much too big for us here.
But I should like to suggest that this class will survive those
who have buried it in words. It has from Tudor times on
showed, in contrast with most continental ruling classes,
an extraordinary ability to absorb able men from lower
classes, and what is even more uncommon, to slough off
in the course of a few generations its most incapable members. Above all, it has managed to take in good time ideas
and programs from intellectuals without ceasing to feel
quite superior to intellectuals, and indeed distrustful of
them. The distrust, however, has rarely degenerated into
hatred, as in parallel circumstances it seems rather om-
inously to be doing right now in the United States. The
old managers and the new planners may yet pull Britain
through in a rather odd and very British partnership.

France is at least as complex a whole as Britain, and, in
spite of much that we two great heirs of the Enlightenment of the eighteenth century have in common, rather
harder for an American to get at intuitively. Yet even the
superficial observer who knew something of the France of

the Twenty Years' Truce—and earlier—can see how much of the older France survives in 1953. It is true that, though the fact has somehow not been as well publicized as the British "revolution by consent," there has been a leveling process in France in the last few generations which has made that country, too, a welfare state. It is almost as hard to keep up a great country estate in France as in England; the French upper and middle classes, contrary to a notion unfortunately widespread in the United States, are heavily taxed. It is the peasant who commonly dodges the income tax, in part at least. The taxes go not only to rearmament, but to social services, among which are relatively generous family allowances and child-welfare services which may help to justify my subjective impression that French children, though like American children they may ulti- mately suffer from having been objects of child worship (may I coin the word *pedolatry?*), look nowadays par- ticularly healthy and happy.

What I wish to emphasize here is that France, though undergoing the leveling process apparently universal in Western society, preserves something of her old and very complex social stratification. Like us, and unlike the British, Frenchmen have committed themselves in the high regions of political faith to the proposition that all men are created equal. Many more in France than in America do indeed question that faith, but in both countries equality has sunk into the common ways beneath the noble beliefs. All Frenchmen are "Monsieur" just as all Americans are "Mac" or at least "Hey, you." I sometimes feel none of us will live to see the day when all Englishmen are, with the small "s," "sir." In France this equality, which is, as

I have suggested by my illustration, an equality of politeness, is crisscrossed by all sorts of actual differences of status, and furthermore, by a general feeling which hardly exists in the United States, that some sort of status, even family status involving heredity, is in the order of nature. I am aware that I have produced a paradox, after warning against the dangers of paradox. But this means merely that I am puzzled about the matter. Somehow the Frenchman comes closer in ordinary life than the rest of us Westerners to accepting with that kind of incomplete resignation we call irony the fact that the ideal is not the real. Even in the service industries—hotels, restaurants, domestic services, the travel industry—which put egalitarian ideals to one of their hardest tests, Frenchmen seem proud of doing a good job. This pride, which quite without ironic overtones used also to be evident in corresponding stations in life in England, I think does show signs of diminishing there.

But we are getting beyond our depths in social psychology. There is, I think, some relation between this French willingness to accept the limitation of this world and that very important fact of French life I have already brought up— French addiction to the small enterprise, the small farm, the family business, their reluctance, in spite of striking exceptions in steel and in a few other industries, to go all out for large-scale industry after the model set by the United States, Germany, Britain, and Russia. At any rate, this addiction to smallness, to "individualism" if you like, is one of the things that endures in France, so much so that the Communists there have had to pretend in their propaganda that Communism is designed especially to protect the peasant-proprietor and the small shopkeeper.

The Survival of Individualism

The fact is that a good deal of what American liberals scornfully, and American businessmen praisefully, call "rugged individualism" persists all over Western Europe even in these days of the welfare state. I propose to take up in conclusion some examples of this survival in business and in intellectual life.

There is little doubt that it is more difficult for the born entrepreneur to get a start in the modern West than it used to be. Yet even in our own day Mr. Howard Johnson has had a Horatio Alger career, starting on a shoestring with a neighborhood icecream business in suburban Boston. The British analogue to Mr. Johnson is a man named Butlin, who from modest beginnings has built up a chain of holiday camps which are—I hope—the last word in mass catering. There seems to be everything—except the possibility of a quiet life—in these Butlin camps. The vacationer gets a standard, uniformly priced package of delights, all provided automatically. A Butlin resort must indeed seem to the sensitive intellectual evidence that perhaps the George Orwell who wrote *1984* was after all a realist, but the point I wish to make is that these halls of regimented pleasure are no product of government planning, but of private business initiative.

Indeed, the Europeans are by no means as far behind us in providing new material comforts for the unvanished middle classes as we often think they are. The Hôtel du Rhone in Geneva, opened in 1951, by no means a hotel de luxe, but aimed rather at the kind of clientele our Statler hotels are aimed at, is a model of unobtrusive modernity, from its ventilation system to its synthetic floor covering, a kind of superlinoleum on which one almost floats. During the last war a colleague and I were able to rent in London a small house which not only had an electric refrigerator and a silex coffeepot, but a central heating system that really worked. We couldn't of course boost the living room up to American standards, which I take to be about blood-heat, but we could get it up almost to 70 degrees Fahrenheit. Though I may be overdoing the role of children in contemporary France, I cannot resist bringing up here the *salon de l'enfance* held yearly in the Grand Palais in Paris. This exhibition is a triumph of ingenuity in the business of providing amusement and perhaps also instruction for the child. There are all sorts of toys and gadgets, all sorts of plans for a better childhood. Even American children would find something new there.

In another field there is the postwar blossoming of the Italian moving-picture industry. A benevolent government has no doubt helped that blossoming, but on the whole it has been the work of private initiative, and I think I am justified in taking over the approved Hollywood term, "industry." Perhaps, like other periods of successful effort in any art, this flowering has come about chiefly through the presence of a few gifted individuals. We are still so ignorant of all that makes for such a flowering that we may be justified in calling the coming-together of such gifted individuals "accidental." Still, we must suspect that there are some social factors behind this sort of achievement. My point is that from war-torn and poverty-stricken Italy there have come better motion pictures—and incidentally better novels —than from the apparently prosperous Italy of Mussolini.

One could cite many more evidences of the continued ability of Western Europeans to produce something new, to create. The recent rise of the West German economy, which I have not witnessed at first hand, is a clear example of the persistence in the mixed economy of those factors of individual inventiveness and enterprise which we are often told were extinguished as early as 1914. But I must pass on to matters more purely of the spirit.

It is very difficult to analyze the temper of one's own time, especially with respect to those signs of decay and death which preoccupy a Spengler, a Sorokin, or a Toynbee. A Roman prophet of doom like Tacitus, we now see, was in part right. But the difficulty is that there are always prophets of doom. It is worth saying again: optimism and pessimism among intellectuals and the intellectual classes are not chemical elements, and they cannot be readily measured. Anyone with an elementary training in historical research and a good library at his disposal could put together, starting with Plato and the Hebrew prophets, an almost continuous chain of quotations like those from Lewis Mumford, T. S. Eliot, and Katherine Anne Porter with which I began this study. There might be occasional gaps during the period of the so-called Dark Ages, for lack of surviving records, but by and large it is true that in every Western generation some articulate person has announced that his is the worst of possible worlds, that his society is sick unto death. The specific details of their complaints do indeed vary, as do their remedies—for, though some of our modern philosophers of history rather gloss over this fact, almost all of them do have remedies to propose, cherish carefully some hopes even for this lost world.

Yet very few of us can see history as a dead-level of unchanging reality beneath a mere froth of change, or else a mere tidal ebb and flow. Something which, with the pro-

viso that we are using a certain kind of metaphor, I am willing to call death, happened to Periclean Athens. All I really
wish to maintain now is that kind of death has not yet happened to Western Europe, and that there are no unmistak-
able signs that kind of death is about to happen there.
Something is happening, which may be no more than a
change of life; and it is happening very slowly, as it must
in that ill-understood organism—again a metaphor—we call
society. The old Europe is still alive, and nowhere more
clearly than in that great variety of ideas about the meaning
of life I have called its multanimity.

Some years ago I was talking over his thesis subject with
Mr. Alan Brown, now president of Hobart and William
Smith Colleges. The thesis, since published, dealt with the
Metaphysical Society, an informal group of distinguished
mid-Victorians which met for dinner and high discussion.
We were discussing its very broad membership, how it
numbered Roman Catholics like Manning and Ward, An-
glicans like Thirlwall and Gladstone, Unitarians like Mar-
tineau, Comtian positivists like Frederic Harrison, agnostics
like T. H. Huxley, indeed a whole spectrum of English
attitudes toward the ultimates. All these men met together
in friendliness and outspoken frankness over a good dinner
in a famous London restaurant. At one point Mr. Brown
remarked parenthetically, "Of course, you can't imagine
anything like that today." He was indeed right in the main.
There is a bitterness in our contemporary intellectual differences, perhaps also a desire for publicity, which works
against so quiet a gathering. We are not all of us quite so
sure as were the Victorians that metaphysics is worth all
that trouble. These and many many other factors, of great
concern to the intellectual historian, militate against just

such a society today, even in England, where high debate still rules in common room and—somewhat muted and mixed with less high matters—also over the air-waves of the British Broadcasting Corporation.

Yet I am sure Mr. Brown did not mean that the great debate does not go on in our way by other means, and with almost as much range and freedom. For it certainly does so continue, heightened by the fact that many of its participants, now as then, engage in it with the fond hope that some day soon it will end in agreement as all men embrace the true faith. We know that the debate goes on here in America, even though Lord Russell and other interested persons tell the world that no one in the United States dares say what he thinks, unless he agrees with, say, Senator Taft —or was it Senator McCarthy? Americans—and incidentally, Frenchmen in modern times—appear always to have lacked the equanimity that made the British Metaphysical Society possible. Nowhere in the West, however, is the debate silenced, and nowhere does it seem yet to be the kind of struggle in which the political victors are determined to silence their opponents in death. In Russia, the debate was just such a deadly struggle, which is in part why it has ended there, for the time at least. In Western Europe it is very much alive. There are indeed totalitarians of both Right and Left in Europe who would end it, totalitarians who enjoy the paradoxical freedom we believers in the endless debate seem bound by our very belief to give them. There are unquestionably such believers in totalitarian solutions in the United States. But they have not won the day in Western Europe, nor here, and I do not think they are winning it. Our *habits* of actual diversity of opinion on high matters and low are perhaps even stronger than our *faith* in its theoretical desirability, which is surely one reason why the heart of the West, Western Europe, most of the Americas, most of Western society overseas elsewhere have not gone totalitarian. Habit is a more important ally of ours than the rationalist liberal likes to admit. Nowhere in Western Europe is habit yet on the side of the totalitarian state and society.

Here I may risk making a proposition perhaps dangerously optimistic. I think it possible that even were the Gaullist Right or the Communist Left to gain control in France, even were English socialists to try to realize the thinly disguised enlightened despotism always threatening in England from Bentham through the old Fabians to the new—even in these unlikely cases I suspect some freedom of speech, some diversity, some of the old Adam as centuries of multanimity in Europe have shaped him would survive, and would eventually wreck the attempt at totalitarian control. You may remember how during the war and the Vichy regime in France many Frenchmen insisted that the new model France had to have the proper one-party organization. The difficulty was that there were so many of these *partis uniques*—at least three major ones and a number of minor ones.

To the quality of this intellectual life in Western Europe I shall return in my last chapter. It may be degenerate, and may deserve those ingenious and often searching epithets Mr. Arnold Toynbee has drawn from his vast knowledge of Greco-Roman culture—schism in the soul, archaism, futurism, pammixia, and proletarianization. Again I call attention to the difficulty that at once arises if you take high culture, and particularly the arts, as measures of the age and health of a society. A list parellel to the list I suggested of

thinkers sure that their own period was hopelessly degenerate could be drawn up, certainly for the last few centuries, numbering critics sure that the then modern art
meant the end of the road, a dissolution of all the decencies
and the beauties. An English critic about 1810 remarked
that Beethoven might fool his own countrymen, but that
Englishmen knew him for a charlatan. My own favorite is
the Boston legend that when Symphony Hall was built in
1904 a conservative outraged by modernism suggested that
instead of "exit" there be inscribed "this way out in case
of—Brahms!"

All I wish to establish now is the fact that the old variety
of views and tastes still obtains in Western Europe. The
academicians still struggle with the *avant-garde*. Heartbreak
House—its heart actually I think in rather better shape than
it used to be in the old Bloomsbury days—still looks scornfully and wistfully toward a Horseback Hall no longer in
its best days, but still riding to the hounds. Positivism,
materialism, secularism, and all their variants, after having
been buried by their profounder enemies in a suitably shal-
low grave, turn out to be quite alive. Christianity, which
the positivists had buried a bit earlier, has of course per-
sisted, and indeed gained as it usually does at the end of a
great war.

I shall not attempt here a survey of the richness of contemporary cultural life in Western Europe. Even Mr.
Shirer, however, somewhat existentially seeks to rally his
reader by remarking of *Midcentury Journey*, "If you come
along with me on this midcentury journey, you will feel
proud and glad, I think, as I did, despite the tribulations
which beset us all, to be living at this tumultuous time in
so great an age." This may not be a true *Blütezeit*, a high

point in cultural history. But if Europe really is sunk in decay, it is certainly not a somnolent decay. I would not question Mr. T. S. Eliot's high place in the line of prophets and witnesses that begins with Plato. Perhaps the world will end, as he says in lines now safely in the anthologies, "not with a bang but a whimper." To me at least it looks as if contemporary Europe were indulging in many more bangs than whimpers—making, in fact, so much noise that one is reminded rather of a nursery than of a death ward.

The Possible Future

European Union

I have in the last two chapters insisted that Western Europe today is, in spite of the horrors of our time, as a whole materially richer than ever before; this is a verifiable fact of the external world, even if we verify through statistics. I have also maintained that one who knew Europe thirty years ago will quite readily recognize Europe today, that the past of Europe is in part also its present. This statement too is reasonably verifiable. Finally, I have said that Europe seems to me alive rather than dead, even in a sense youthful rather than senile. That is of course a private judgment.

I come in this last chapter to a set of problems where no man's answers can be more than guesses. I shall write about the possible future of Western Europe, and shall emphasize the new rather than the old. But I trust I shall be building on the firm ground of the old, the known, the established.

The most important new thing in Western Europe would be some greater actual union, some effective political, or at least economic, integration of the whole or part of the region. Now the voluntary successful union in a common state, a common government, of any contemporary European countries would be a revolution more striking than any of the innumerable revolutions of morals, taste, politics, and science our publicists have noted, or perhaps imagined, in the last few decades. No such voluntary union has taken place there since the mid-nineteenth century unification of Italy and Germany—and to many historians those national unifications seem more forced than voluntary. We Americans must be especially careful not to let our hopes simplify our thinking about European political unity, and especially not to let that simplification take this form, so irritating to Europeans: we Americans got together in the eighteenth century, so you people ought to be able to get together now.

Several kinds of functional coöperative undertakings among the states of Western Europe seem to me to be among the possible futures of the region. No political union, no federal union to produce a *Bundesstaat*, or true federal state, seems to me to be among the possible futures. Here indeed I assume a future of a generation or so, a future which for many of us will someday be a present. What Europe will be like a century or two from now, or a millennium from now, is a perfectly legitimate subject for speculation, but it is not one that concerns me now. The human beings, leaders and led, who would in our days have to make and carry out the decisions to create a West European state are in my opinion quite unable to make and carry out these decisions. Their past performances—and history can be at least a kind of form-sheet—show that they cannot go much faster than they are now going. Full European union, or even such a union as that of Belgium, Netherlands, and Luxembourg into a single new state, would be like asking a top-notch miler today to cut thirty seconds or so off his time, which is impossible. Note that I use a human runner, not a motorcar or an airplane, as my example. Men

are not machines, even if advanced eighteenth-century
thinkers like La Mettrie thought them so. Darwinism here
reinforces Christianity on one important point: man is not
perfectible within the time-scale of human technology.

I realize very well that on this as on so many problems
people's minds tend to be made up—as mine clearly is—and
that facts, statistics, and metaphors no matter how skillfully
marshaled will not change our minds for many of us. The
European federationist can get quite different results from
my own figure of speech. The miler, he would say, doesn't
need to make any such fantastic advance as cutting thirty
seconds off his time: all he needs to do is set a new record
for himself; and for that all he needs is the best track the
experts can build, and the will and the heart to go after the
record. The most hopeful federationist might push aside
as irrelevant all my figure of speech except that of speed
and say: we aren't dealing with unaided human muscles, but
with man's amazing ability to use his brains to get beyond
his muscles; national sovereignty and the United Nations
are horse-and-buggy; we've got the fine internal combus-
tion engine of World Government right at hand; all we
have to do is crank it up, and off we go.

I probably haven't done very well in my attempt to see
the other fellow's point of view. The World Federationists,
even the European Unionists, will feel that I have carica-
tured them. So we had better leave the matter here, and pro-
ceed to a much more concrete matter, the actual ways in
which Europeans *are* trying to work together, the ways in
which they are actually getting beyond the sovereign
nation-state in practice. The sum total of these ways is
impressive, quite enough to persuade me that the most
likely future for Western Europe lies in the attempt to make

existing methods of coöperation more effective, and in exploring the possibility of adding new ways.

First of all, almost all of the Western European nations are part of the United Nations. Now to a historian the United Nations seem to be in pretty direct succession to the League of Nations of 1919, the Congress System of 1815, and the Concert of Europe of the early eighteenth century, to go no further back. The pessimist may say these attempts to organize peace, occurring as they do after particularly severe general or world wars, are no more than the drunkard's morning-after repentance and of no more lasting significance. The optimist may say that these attempts to organize peace are the conscious efforts of the sounder parts of society to rally the recuperative forces of men in society after the disasters of war, and that on the whole they show over the centuries a slow but appreciable progress. I find myself agreeing with the optimist, who is surely no very wild one if he finds the United Nations of 1953 an improvement over the alliance system of the early eighteenth century. The United Nations may be basically no more than a gathering of diplomatists, and it certainly is not a government, not a superstate. But it is an elaborately organized set of institutions, staffed by trained specialists, and at the very least it channels disputes, provides possibilities of settlement. It has obviously and almost miraculously to some of us what the League of Nations had not, the wholehearted participation of the American government and of the majority of the American people.

Then there is the so-called Schuman Plan, which has now begun operations. Six West European countries, France, the three countries of Benelux, West Germany, and Italy, have actually undertaken to set up a joint authority which has constitutional power to make and enforce laws binding on all six countries. Its power is limited to two closely related industries, iron and coal, together with the materials and equipment necessary to make steel. But it is fair to say that in respect to one specific field of government activity, these six countries have agreed to give up part of their "sovereignty." In a limited field, the new coal and steel authority really seems to be supranational, to be a *Bundesstaat* or true federal state, not just a *Staatenbund*, or league of states. The authority, on paper at least, really has authority. It remains to see whether the plan will work. Its governing body is almost certain to make sooner or later a decision so unpalatable to one of the member states that the government of that state will refuse to accept the decision. We must not set too high our hopes for this pioneering attempt to get beyond the nation-state. Given reasonably stable world economic conditions, it has I think a chance of getting consolidated enough to stand the strains it will have to face. A depression, or even a serious recession, may quite possibly wreck it before it has a chance to establish itself as a going concern. But the mere fact that the Schuman Plan is being given a trial shows that West Europe has not lost the ability to make—and make by agreement arrived at by discussion—a major political experiment. This does look like something other than a patient turning over in his sickbed.

NATO, the North Atlantic Treaty Organization, is another experiment in international organization for regular, disciplined action, not merely for consultation and coöperation. The historian is bound to see in this organization basically a military coalition of the kind that has always come into being when the balance of power in our state-system is as sharply defined as it is by the present rivalry between the United States and Russia. But it is already, and if plans for a European army work out it will be even more, a much tighter military coalition than we have ever had at comparable periods in the history of our Western state-system, which is now in fact a world-system. This is a danger, but it is also a promise. There is in the development of international military organization the same tendency to a closer and more efficient working together—still well short of perfect communion—we have noted in diplomatic organization. NATO, like the United Nations, is at least a better piece of machinery than its forerunners of the eighteenth century, better than earlier models. I have always cherished the story, which like most such stories is very hard to establish as true, that in the first campaigns against revolutionary France in 1792 the allied armies of Prussia and Austria were so mutually distrustful that they commonly set out sentries each against the other as well as against the French. In the war of 1914–1918 a unified high command was not achieved on the Western front until the last moment, and there was never a single Allied army. In this last war we and the British achieved an extraordinary interleaving of staffs not only in planning but in the field. There were difficulties, but they were overcome, sometimes in the way indicated by one of the folk stories about General Eisenhower. The general is said to have relieved an American officer of his command, not because the officer called his British subordinate a son-of-a-bitch, but because he called him a *British* son-of-a-bitch. In NATO we are trying to pick up where we left off at the end of the war, and not altogether without success. We should not be too impatient with the French if they slow up, or even prevent, the achievement of a fully integrated European army. A NATO army even with separable national units that hung together as well as did Eisenhower's in 1944 would in itself be a remarkable achievement.

There is also the Council of Europe, which unlike the Schuman Plan Organization, NATO, and indeed some of the functional carry-overs from the League of Nations, is so far an affair of words rather than deeds. The Council of Europe was founded on May 5, 1949. Its foundation members were Belgium, Denmark, France, Ireland, Italy, Luxembourg, the Netherlands, Norway, Sweden, and the United Kingdom. Western Germany and the Saar became associate members, with right of representation in the Consultative Assembly only, in 1950. The seat of the Council is at Strasbourg in Alsace. It is not by any means a wholly unofficial pressure group of propagandists and planners, like the numerous groups organized throughout the West for Union Now, World Federation, and the like. The Council itself is composed of the Foreign Ministers of the member states. The Consultative Assembly, delegates to which are appointed as each member state wishes, is for the most part composed of deputies from the respective parliamentary bodies. There is a professional secretariat. The debates in the Assembly are public, and are reported in the major newspapers.

The Council has announced that its work is supplementary to, and in no sense an undermining of, the work of the United Nations and other established international bodies. It is certainly, in the minds of such influential sponsors as Sir Winston Churchill and M. Paul Reynaud, a preliminary to a real European union. One of the best brief accounts of its work is the final chapter of M. Paul Reynaud's *Unite or*

Perish, published in English in New York in 1951. A plan
for a closer political union of the six nations of the Schuman
Plan—France, West Germany, Italy, the Netherlands, Belgium, and Luxembourg—has recently been passed unani-
mously at Strasbourg. It has not at this writing in midsum-
mer of 1953 become a reality, and it may not for some time.
Britain, at least, is apparently somewhat more benevolent
toward the Council than toward the Schuman Plan.

It would be premature to hail in Strasbourg the European
equivalent of our Philadelphia Convention of 1787, from
which emerged the present Constitution of the United
States of America. A United States of Europe—even of
Western, democratic Europe—will be very hard indeed to
found. But they are making a conscious beginning of the
task at Strasbourg. Men actually engaged responsibly in the
work of governing their own countries—politicians, if the
word doesn't offend you—are at work in the Council of
Europe, and not merely publicists, political scientists, propagandists. Experience suggests that if the job is to be done,
politicians have to do it. There were politicians at work in
Philadelphia in 1787.

Finally, there is the Saar. Last July the German Bundes-
tag firmly announced that the Saar must be part of Germany. The French, apparently, would be content with an
autonomous Saarland, even a "Europeanized" Saarland, tied
economically to France. No sensible commentator would
risk a firm prognosis here. The Saar may prove to be the
specific case that keeps Germany and France divided; or
it may be the specific case on which hinges the whole process of reconciliation between these old enemies. This tiny
but rich coal region, highly industrialized, and German by
language and tradition, is a fascinating test case. For if the

Saar is, quite literally, German at heart, its economic interests as the world now is lie very clearly in free trade with
France. Rarely are emotions and interests, heart and head,
so neatly opposed in this world. We should at least learn
something about the relative importance of these contrary
pulls on a human group from what happens in the Saar in
the near future. Much more hopeful we cannot be. Heaven
on earth is not likely to start in the Saar.

I wrote earlier that our American success in getting beyond the little red one-room schoolhouse to the graded district school might throw light on the problem of greater
union among West European states. We Americans have
reformed the rural school system; we have not reformed
the whole system of rural local government. In a democracy, those reforms get through behind which there are concrete interests and enthusiasms as well as abstract ideas and
ideals. I realize I am making a hasty generalization, begging,
in a way, a question which is at the heart of social psychology. Perhaps I had better rest with my concrete comparisons. The Schuman Plan, and some of the functional organi-
zations of the United Nations, seem to me like the district
school plan, practical; total union for all Western Europe
in our time seems to me like a plan for total reform of our
local government—or better yet, like Mr. W. Y. Elliott's
ingenious plan for cutting down the number of our forty-
eight—or forty-nine—states, impractical.

I have hitherto been working on the evident, if unstated,
assumption that for the kind of world most of us Americans
want some stronger union of Western Europe is desirable
as a long-term aim. I do indeed think that such a union
would help make the kind of world we want. But a historian

addicted to the Machiavellian view, to what is often called realism, would have to warn that a Europe—even the truncated Europe we have been calling "Western Europe"— might, if by some miracle it could be forged into a really united state, turn out to be a rival, even an enemy. Such a state, especially if by retaining some at least of the overseas possessions of existing states like Britain, France, and Belgium it had access to important raw materials, would be as much a superpower as the United States or the USSR. It would have a greater population than either, and an industrial potential quite as great. No such state seems to me possible in our own time, but the remote possibility that it might arise should not in the least deter us from trying to help the formation of a West European union.

In our Western state-system those states in the past which have attained the kind of leadership or hegemony we Americans now have, seem always to have pursued a policy of "divide and rule." This is certainly true even of one of the best of them, Victorian England. "Divide and rule" is an easy, in a sense a natural, policy, a policy which has been at the root of the balance-of-power principle. It has helped to preserve our system of nation-states from imperial domination, helped to preserve a concrete territorial and material basis for the spiritual good as well as for the bad in what we call nationalism; but it has also prevented any federal union transcending that system and its major evil, war. I think we have got to gamble on a possible union of Europe as a step in transcending the politics of balance of power, as a step to a distant but not impossible world government based on the federal, not the imperialist, principle, on consent, not on force.

The Economic Future

I come now to the possible economic future of Western Europe. I have already stated the basic economic problem that confronts the area: how to support in the style to which they have become accustomed and which they will not willingly abandon, some fifty, perhaps a hundred, millions of people for whom food and other basic raw materials do not exist within the area, and cannot by existing means be produced there. We are concerned with the reasonable future of a generation or two. It is perhaps conceivable that the chemists, who have already done wonders, will do something really astounding, such as making cellulose digestible for human beings. Even then, I expect that many Englishmen would insist that the oaks of England were not designed for eating. Seriously, though scientific agriculture, technology, and good administration can add something to the food and other raw material resources of Western Europe, though new sources of power in the region may be found, it is clear that Western Europe will have to live in the immediate future as it has lived in the past few centuries, by exchanging finished goods and services for food and other raw materials.

This means that somewhere else on earth people will have to send food and raw materials to Western Europe and accept finished goods and services in return; or, to drive home the obvious, it means that somewhere outside of Europe there must be areas which are not economically autarkic, which produce more food, oil, rubber, metals and other raw materials than they need, and less machinery, textiles, ships, other finished goods, banking and insurance than they need. Now, once more talking about a measurable future, not a far-distant one, I think we can find right within our own borders evidence that within a given great free-trading area, an old industrial region far more deprived than even Western Europe of food and raw materials can do very well for itself. There is the story, unquestionably Californian in origin, about the Californian who remarked that if the United States had been settled in the opposite direction, from the Pacific Coast instead of from the Atlantic, New England would still be a howling wilderness. But the country was settled from the Atlantic side. New England, shut off completely from the rest of the world, would starve even more quickly than would Old England so shut off. And indeed the prophets of doom have been killing off New England for at least a century. But, though New England is not booming like Texas, Yankees are very far from starving. Iowa farmers still buy New England cotton goods, even though they buy more cotton goods from the Piedmont, and they buy Yankee household appliances; and Yankees still enjoy Iowa corn-fed pork.

Of course if Iowa and other parts of the country could build trade barriers against New England, if each American region could and did try to be self-sufficient, we in New England could not carry on as we are doing. Within a free-trading area the classical economic doctrine of comparative advantage still holds. If there were, not the absolute free trade Cobden and his fellows preached, but some approximation to free trade over large parts of the world, then I think it obvious that Old England, for example, could hold its own at least as well as New England has. It is still cheaper to produce knives in Sheffield than in Australia, and cheaper to produce mutton in Australia than in Yorkshire.

There is, even in our neo-mercantilist world, enough of the old sort of international trade so that, with some help from us in the form of what are really subsidies, Western Europe has been able to keep going, as we have seen, on a relatively high standard of living. If America can convert those subsidies to trade, if, to be concrete, we can abstain from developing all our industrial capacities for the sake of a world balance, then Europe will be well on the way to recovery. Even more important would be the lifting of trade restrictions within the British Commonwealth and the French Union, in South America, and elsewhere. The experts are working toward this goal, and though it is a goal which public opinion finds it hard to get excited about —economics will probably never quite live down that tag, the "dismal science"—it is surely a goal of major importance, and one toward which American energies should be directed.

In the short term, at least, I think we should soften as much as we can our intransigeant attitude toward what is left of European colonialism. Even on idealistic grounds, it seems clear that the too rapid emancipation of regions like Central Africa, Madagascar, Malaya is no kindness to native populations. The topic is one on which, like many we have touched upon here, emotional balance is hard to attain. The metaphor of "middle of the road" may be given a twist that makes it most unsatisfactory. It is not, in the presence of traffic, a good place to drive. Yet on this specific problem, few indeed would really sympathize with Robespierre's famous outburst, when in debate it was brought out that the French sugar islands in the Caribbean were peopled largely by blacks not ready for the practice of Liberty, Equality, Fraternity, that immediate wholesale emancipation of the blacks would be disastrous. No matter, cried Robespierre, "let the colonies perish rather than a principle!"

Now if the English got out of Malaya, the French out of Indo-China, if all the European countries got out of Africa, the consequences would probably not be just what they were when the French got out of—were driven out of—Haiti. You may even argue that it was better for the Haitians to undergo the tragic history that has been theirs since 1789 as free men than to have been nursed along even by a benevolent France. Yet in no very good sense were they free men under Christophe or Dessalines, or under the corrupt rule of their nineteenth-century presidents. We nursed the Filipinos for half a century before we cut them loose—and even so, they must have our "protection" for some time to come.

The British and the French in their different ways are both trying to preserve some degree of tutelage over their black and brown dependents. It is a hard task for them to alter the past of exploitation. The very sore spot of Kenya points up the difficulty, for in Kenya the whites have the best lands, and the blacks, who are multiplying under conditions of public law and public health at least far better than in the past, have not enough land for themselves. Perhaps the Mau Mau, like the blacks in Haiti, should be allowed to drive out the white landowners. But again, a Kenyan Christophe—no unlikely thing—is not a prospect even the "liberal" should contemplate happily.

Actually no one region like Kenya is wholly typical. The whites never have become farmers or grazers in the lowlands of tropical Africa. Tribal organization may there be modernized into effective modern self-government. The

whole Near East, including French North Africa, is far
too advanced already in nationalism, and in a rudimentary
way in economic life, for sheer nursing along by Europeans.
Malaya presents the special problem of a large and not yet
assimilated Chinese minority. And so it goes throughout
the old colonial world.

We can but urge patience and an experimental attitude.
The spirit of Robespierre must not be ours. Reactionary
elements in Britain and in France certainly would like to go
back simply to their own good old days, but they are not
in power and it is fairly safe to say that in both these great
colonial powers men of good will are struggling with the
problems the past has saddled them with. One may hope
that the precedent of India, Pakistan, and Ceylon, free
nations but not wholly cut off politically from their former
"masters," can be gradually extended, and that the colored
peoples of Africa and southeast Asia will not have to undergo the fate of Haiti.

There is, moreover, a factor present today that was not
present in Haiti in the nineteenth century. We have come
to realize that when Western Europeans step out of Asiatic
"colonial" areas, Eastern Europeans—Russians—step in, directly or through their native stooges. We have even apparently decided for the present to support wicked France
in her colony of Indo-China. But even were Russian pressure somewhat relieved, I do not think we should urge on
Western Europe a too hasty abandonment of what is left
of the colonial system. We must not forget the upperdog
in concern for the underdog. In this imperfect world, some
temporary maintenance of this system may well make the
difference between the survival of a strong and prosperous
Western Europe and its dangerous economic weakening.

And economic weakening of Western Europe is almost certain to lead to grave political disturbances there. Europe is still the place where the big wars, the bad wars, start.

If Western Europe's economic future depends in part on the maintenance of an exchange of European manufactured goods and services for overseas food and raw materials, it depends in the longer run on the maintenance of Western Europe's comparative advantage—that is, on the region's ability to produce for export goods which overseas regions will prefer to what they might produce themselves. There are many economic measures of this kind of advantage— measures of cost and productivity; I have deliberately put the matter in terms of overseas demand for European goods, if only to remind you that the ultimate consumers count.

For those who believe that the kind of industrial productivity needed to maintain Western Europe's export markets is directly measured by the closeness with which a given society approaches standards set by Herbert Spencer's *Social Statics* and *The Man vs. the State*, Western Europe is pretty far gone on the road to extinction. These believers in dogmatic laissez faire are by no means limited to the United States. There are Englishmen who hold that theirs is an ill-fare not a welfare state, Frenchmen who think their government far-gone in socialism. But we must not allow ourselves to get involved in the general problem of whether the increasing use of government intervention to achieve higher incomes for the poorer classes is the road to serfdom and ruin. Such use of government, whether or not you label it socialism, collectivism, the welfare state, or even New Deal or Fair Deal, has been universal in the West, though varying greatly in different countries. I think that on the whole the account I have already given shows that such use of government intervention in Western Europe has not prevented a very high degree of economic recovery in the years since the war. For the immediate future, if we give up oversimple and overabstract debates as to the virtues and vices of socialism or individualism and concentrate on what seems likely to happen in Western Europe, we shall conclude that there are good chances of economic survival.

There is no chance that anywhere in Western Europe men will go back to Herbert Spencer, to formulas like "that government governs best which governs least, and least expensively." Social-security measures of many kinds, government ownership and operation of railways and some major heavy industries, price controls and regulation of all sorts will be the rule not only in England and Sweden, but to a degree in all Western Europe. But, unless all signs fail, this will not mean an extinction of human ability to invent, to improve, to work effectively. It will not mean a dead level of stagnation, if only because the kind of collectivism that has grown up in the modern Western world has not in fact turned out to be the simple bureaucratic formula nineteenth-century critics of collectivist ideas thought "socialism" in practice would be.

One of the actual forms the economic development of Europe is increasingly taking is that of the public corporation, a form which already has many variants in different countries. The public corporation is in part at least the result of an effort by its planners to avoid the evils so often predicted of socialism—bureaucratic methods, subordination to the whims of politics, lack of team spirit, lack of initiative. The public corporation is a genuine corporation in something like the old medieval sense; that is, it is a corporate group with a life of its own, a sphere of action, an independence based on rights—the rights set up in its charter. Whether it can in a pinch maintain those rights against a government will no doubt be decisively tested somewhere before long. Certainly the rights of the public corporation are not unlimited, in Great Britain, for instance. They are certainly less than, by the precedent of the Dartmouth College case and much more constitutional law, we assume in America are the rights of any private corporation. But they are not inexistent; these public corporations are not just the creatures of the government.

On the whole the history of one of the best known of these corporations shows that they can indeed have a life, a spirit of their own. The British Broadcasting Corporation has often been reproached with excessive timidity, with a desire not to offend politicians, with self-righteously seeking to improve public tastes, and with also catering to the low tastes of the public. In short, radio in Britain, where it is in the hands of a public corporation, and radio in the United States, where it is in the hands of a few private corporations, seems to arouse much the same sort of reactions among the people of the two countries. I do not wish to deny that there are differences between the radio fare in the two countries, but, even though in Britain you do not have the advertising dinned in your ear, I am much more struck with the similarities. I grant you that in this country individuals have made money out of the actual process of broadcasting and that in England they have not, although the BBC is of course not a drain on the Exchequer. Moreover, it is sometimes forgotten that in Britain the actual manufacture of radio and television equipment is in private hands, a good deal of it in the hands of a great international corporation, that of Phillips. But it is surely striking that in both the

United States and in Britain the last thirty years have seen the successful rise to a prominent place in the economy of a great new industry of radio and television.

British nationalization has in general taken a form that may be described rather as a public corporation than as a simple government "department," like the Post Office. Coal mining, and indeed the distribution of coal, is now a monopoly, a nationalized industry. It has, incidentally, to face the competition of oil and electricity, so it is not quite the monopoly that horrified some classical economists. The management is unified in a central board, but the actual administration is broken down by regions which have at least the autonomy of any organized group in real life. For in real life the absolutely perfect chain of command, the push-button organization, simply does not exist. Management and labor are still true groups; there are still unions, and as a matter of fact, still strikes in the British coal industry. The managers are indeed no longer responsible to stockholders, but it is a commonplace nowadays that they are not so responsible in any immediate sense in capitalist societies. The managers of the British coal industry are indeed responsible to the government, are appointed by the government. But the fact is that they are still essentially recruited by and among themselves; they are not politicians. We need not go all the way with Mr. James Burnham's *Managerial Revolution* to recognize that the modern corporation, in the United States as in Britain, is no longer the simple one-man affair of the classical entrepreneur. The coal industry in Britain is a vast corporation, free indeed from the pressure to make a profit for stockholders, but otherwise facing the necessity—including the necessity of meeting competition of other corporations offering other fuels to the consumer—of producing and marketing its product efficiently. It starts with serious handicaps—an obsolescent plant, a lack of an abundant, easily worked supply of coal, and a past of bad labor relations. It has not worked the miracles some British socialists hoped for and expected, but it has not failed dismally as some conservatives were sure it would fail. It has, in short, proved to be a corporation with a life of its own.

Americans, save for the economic die-hards, have indeed been better disposed toward our own best-known example of the public corporation. The TVA has had an amazingly good press, both here and abroad. Europeans who come to this country are most eager to see this specimen of American enterprise in a new form. Yet TVA would have shocked Herbert Spencer—and not only Herbert Spencer. It has, however, clearly kept itself free from the kind of politics the older economists were sure would lame any experiment of the sort. It has not been free of public opinion, has indeed done a very good and very modern job in public relations. One may hope that we can be at least as patient with European attempts to do something of the sort as we have been with the TVA.

Indeed, in this whole matter of modern economic organization the basic problems—how to reconcile size with efficiency, how to reconcile growth and innovation with stability, how to reconcile reward, incentive, indeed at bottom private property, with a high minimal standard of living for everyone—are problems which in the free West we are trying to solve by the methods summed up in the phrase a "mixed economy" and not by the methods of Russian

Communism. This is a common effort, in which we should regard ourselves rather as partners of Western Europe than as rivals, if only because if Europe fails to make a mixed economy work she will be forced to try a communist economy, with disastrous results for us. There is no chance whatever that Western Europe will return to laissez faire. I think, however, that the record of the postwar years shows that barring an immediate general war, Western Europe is on its way to make its mixed economy work.

One of the interesting questions that faces the economist is that of measuring the exact degree of the mixture in a given mixed economy. For one thing, if you seek for a statistical measure of the "free" sector of the economy as distinguished from the "nationalized" or "collectivized" sector, you run up against the fact that there are many degrees of nationalization, from the public corporation like the BBC or that curious French hybrid, the *Régie Renault* which administers the great Renault motor works, taken over at the end of the war because the management had collaborated so completely with the Germans, right down to the Post Office, which is, I take it, a completely "socialistic" institution even in the United States. Moreover, the free sector of the economy is everywhere subject to various forms of government regulation and especially to government fiscal policy. Finally, the present high level of military expenditures takes from all Western nations a large slice of the national income. Omitting these military expenditures it does seem likely that even in the British economy private industry, including of course agriculture, accounts for the lion's share of the gross national product, probably indeed well over sixty per cent, or more. That does not seem to me a danger point.

The Spirit of Western Europe

I come now to the central problem of this book: is the state of mind of the peoples of Western Europe, their "temper," such that they can face with energy and confidence the task of rebuilding, which is really a task of building anew? Or are they really—I get back to the inescapable metaphor with which I began—*old* peoples, unable to make new responses, worn-out mentally and physically, in short, finished, done for. A great many Americans, certainly, make the offhand assumption that Western Europe is finished. I am shocked to find that many of our undergraduates not only think of France as a neg-- ligible factor in world affairs, but are not even aware that France has ever been a leader of civilization. As for Britain, they think of her with a certain degree of *Schadenfreude* as almost wholly dependent on our bounty.

Alluring though the temptation to try to analyze the state of the West in Spenglerian or Toynbean terms may be, I think we must put the temptation behind us. As I have perhaps insisted too much already, we just cannot make the diagnosis of senility or decay in a contemporary society. We cannot even say that if everybody in a given society were in the state of mind of the writers I quoted at the beginning of this book, then that society really is on its last legs. For such a statement would be an absurdity, quite contrary to any possibility, if only because no society is composed solely of intellectuals. It might be less absurd to say that if everybody, or at least the great majority of a society showed by their actual behavior that they despaired utterly of life on this earth, that they had no future, then that society could not exist. But this supposition is as absurd as the first, and makes no sense empirically, not even for that classic example of death-and-decay, the only one in our society we know much about, the break-up of the Roman Empire in the West. For it was the toughness of the millions of people of that Empire, the common people even more than the intellectuals, that enabled them eventually to absorb the German barbarians, and survive. If they had not had that toughness, I should not have been able just now to write "survive," but would have had to write something like "ueberleben."

But I am getting drawn in spite of myself into the vortex of the philosophy of history. That the peoples of Western Europe are not sunk in an almost unthinkable supineness is clear from their re-action—that well-worn tag is really apt, for they did *act*—to Hitler. What the British did we all know; but we all too commonly blame the continental peoples, and especially the French, Belgians, and Dutch, for their collapse in 1940. After all, had there been dry land for Hitler's armies to go as far west as they went east—to Stalingrad—they would have got to what is actually the mid-Atlantic. Western Europe, unfortunately, does not have the space the Russians have. The "collapse" of France in 1940 was, as De Gaulle well said at the time, a defeat in battle. Prussia suffered as bad a defeat by the French at Jena in 1806, was overrun by French cavalry which moved almost as fast as did German motorized troops in 1940, was occupied, and had its collaborators. Yet Prussia was fundamentally sound in 1806, and soon developed its resistance. So, too, the French after the shock of 1940 developed their resistance, which in 1944 gave the Allies very great aid indeed.

I have tried to show that to judge by their actions, by

their actual work, the peoples of Western Europe have displayed since the war a very great ability to come back. But I grant if their activities are, so to speak, merely a set of reflexes, a kind of dogged and unthinking continuance of ways to which they are accustomed, if their activities are uninformed by the kind of adaptive thinking we used to subsume under the concept of "progress," then indeed Europe is as badly off as the pessimists think she is. I do not think the peoples of Western Europe are in anything like this hopeless state of mind.

Now in this broad concluding survey of their actual state of mind I shall somewhat reluctantly make a distinction—not, please note carefully, a clear-cut opposition— between the temper of the intellectuals, the people whose main concern is with words and symbols, and the others, the people whose main concern is with things and their relationships. I say reluctantly because I do not wish to make a false and usually snobbish distinction between intellectual sheep and nonintellectual goats, and because I do not wish to imply that what the artists and thinkers do is quite unrelated to what ordinary people do. But, as we have had to content ourselves with merely skirting the philosophy of history, so we must content ourselves with skirting the even more puzzling subject of the sociology of the intellectual classes. For the present it is enough to note that, for the purposes of a rough analysis of the state of mind of contemporary Western Europeans, a quite undogmatic and flexible empirical distinction between intellectuals and the rest of the people is a convenient tool of thought.

Let us begin with the intellectuals, if only because since they are articulate they are easier, at least on the surface, to get at. I am willing to agree that this is an Age of Anxiety, and that no one is likely, if one can judge by its first half, to write a book about the twentieth century with a title like that the late F. S. Marvin chose for one on the nineteenth, *The Century of Hope.* Yet I think it most important to note that the disciplines from which that metaphor of anxiety stems, psychology, or even psychiatry, are very far indeed from gloom and despair. The psychologist recognizes the existence of anxiety, but he has by no means given up the attempt to overcome it. He does not, if he is sensible, think he can overcome it always and in everybody; but he is no pessimist, nor even in a derogatory sense, an anti-intellectual. Indeed, Freud seems to me the legitimate heir of the wiser and subtler spirits of the eighteenth-century Enlightenment, just as Marx is the legitimate heir of the shallower and more impatient spirits of that century.

The closest thing to a fashionable belief in postwar times has been Existentialism, by no means a rosy, happy outlook on life. The existentialists are split into two wings, the Christian and the non-Christian. The Christian existentialists, in so far as they are Christians, cannot be wholly pessimistic about man's fate. No doubt some of the followers of Kierkegaard, like the master himself, must seem to the moderate, earthly outsider wild Christians, Christians who have tipped toward madness the difficult balance Christianity has always had to maintain between this world of the senses and some other world or worlds. But the bulk of the young people in Western Europe who have been influenced by the undoubted postwar revival of Christian faith—a complex matter, by no means adequately described

as existentialist—seem to me well-balanced, anxious to face
this harsh world serenely, not disposed to flee it.

The non-Christian existentialists, whose great vogue is
French, and whose best-known leaders are Sartre and
Camus, do not seem to me to form a major current in the
thought of our time; but it is an interesting one, in which
I find confirmation of my thesis that the thought of contemporary Western Europe is by no means as pessimistic
as it is painted. To be very summary, these men and women
are Stoics, rather querulous and therefore incomplete
Stoics, but still men and women who refuse to lie down
and be run over, whose very querulousness is a sign of
their fighting spirit. At bottom they enjoy their suffering
—and not really in a perverse sense, but rather in the spirit
of "my head is bloody but unbowed." I suspect that at
moments they may even forget to suffer, if only in the
spirit of the very pessimistic forgotten poet, who once
turned upon himself and wrote:

> *Terence, this is stupid stuff:*
> *You eat your victuals fast enough;*
> *There can't be much amiss, 'tis clear,*
> *To see the rate you drink your beer.*

Moreover, some of the simpler and more hopeful faiths
still survive, in something of the way A. E. Housman, who
of course is not really forgotten, survives. The bright
young men today, as usual when they are so described, for
the most part actually bright middle-aged men, would not
be caught dead with a copy of *A Shropshire Lad*, any
more than those of my generation would have been caught
dead with a copy of *Evangeline*. Almost certainly many

younger people will live to find that the work of T. S.
Eliot has had the same fate among the *avant-garde* of 1980.
But Eliot will survive fashion. What I am saying is that
in a sense the direct heritage of the Enlightenment, the line
of Voltaire and Jefferson, the Utilitarians and the Fabians,
even though it is by no means the height of intellectual
fashion, remains a living heritage. Lord Russell, if no one
else, should remind us how long-lived that tradition is.

Translated into political terms, this survival of the
tradition of the Enlightenment, enriched and deepened as
I think it has been by our modern awareness of the importance of the irrational—or the nonrational—in human
life and therefore of the necessity of gradualness, means
the survival of the Third Force, the Vital Center, the
moderate but firm democrats. The strength of this force
in Britain and in the small countries of Scandinavia, the
Lowlands, and Switzerland is obvious. In Germany, Italy,
and above all France this force is indeed more obviously
menaced by extremists who in power might set our common
cause back seriously. The recent elections in Italy have
weakened it there, but by no means destroyed it. Even in
these countries the moderate democrats have managed to
cling to power ever since the end of the war, and I think
an unbiased observer would conclude that today they are
at least no weaker over the whole region than they were
eight years ago. Certainly Communism has not made
important converts among the intellectuals anywhere in
the West in the last few years—Sartre, contrary to belief
in some quarters, is no better convert than was André Gide
—nor to judge by the election returns, among the whole
population. The high tide would seem for the present to
be passed.

Modern art remains a puzzle to the social diagnostician. Without going all the way with horrified conservatives I am willing to admit that some of the work of the twentieth-century *avant-garde* does seem to me quite beyond the border of sanity, does seem to me a kind of cultivation of private, quite eccentric experience that can never be absorbed into the common experience of educated men. Yet we must not forget that the history of the arts—I am using the word in the widest sense to include literature as well as the arts—is filled with dead ends now known only to historians of the arts. As I suggested earlier, some of the more shocking innovators of the first part of our century are now safely enshrined as classics. Somehow time does sort out, not perhaps with perfect clarity the good from the bad, but at least the communicable from the uncommunicable. The once very cautious French ministry of fine arts, which used never to risk official exhibits of contemporary arts, has now housed on the Avenue du Président Wilson (no, they haven't changed the name) a most interesting collection which comes right down to the day before yesterday. As a mere layman with perhaps too strong a desire not to be illiberal in these matters, I was struck with how much of this work held my interest, seemed indeed to give me the encouraging feeling that I could understand a little of what it was all about. I am quite sure that many paintings and statues there exhibited will not be exhibited in 2053. But much of what was hopefully exhibited in 1853 is fortunately not around to bore or disturb us in 1953. The failures of 1853, I grant you, are not Dadaist or Abstractionist failures. But that is only to say the obvious, that ours is in the arts a more daringly experimental age than was the Victorian. It still seems possible, indeed probable, that some of our experiments have been successful ones. And the dead do not make experiments—not at least of the kind we mortals can analyze here on earth.

In a wider sense than is given by art and literature, the culture of contemporary Western Europe shows a clear vitality, the ability to achieve outstanding, new things. We Americans sometimes take an attitude which infuriates us when we find it among the Russians—that of assuming we have a natural monopoly of the first places in everything from science to sport. This is not so; the list of firsts for Western Europe in our own time is not to be forgotten. It was the British who brought to first fruit radar and the jet airplane, however much we Americans have done to develop them. German inventiveness we are less likely to question, and we have made full use of it since we defeated them.

The French we are likely to dismiss as quite burned out. Yet the French have just set up at Mont-Louis in the Pyrenees the first major pilot plant for the direct use of sun power; and they have just finished at Donzère-Mondragon on the Rhône a great hydroelectric plant which, by diverting the river into a canal, avoids the drowning of good farming land in a great reservoir subject to the difficulties of silting-up. French science has suffered from French economic and political difficulties, as has French scholarship, but neither are at as low an ebb as many Americans assume. French physics and French economics are not at the moment very distinguished; French biology remains at a very high creative level. The "school of Paris" is getting old—most of its painters who are still living are septuagenarians at least—but Paris is still a very great center of painting. Nor has Hollywood, in spite of the claims of

American periodicals, by any means replaced Paris as the center of fashions for women. As for what Hollywood really symbolizes, we need not here repeat the endless complaints of American intellectuals against our moving pictures. Sufficient to note that the Europeans have a lively, interesting movie industry of their own, and that they can sometimes out-Hollywood Hollywood itself, as well as turn out such subtle and wholly unsentimental pictures as the recent French *Jeux Interdits*.

The American who "keeps up with" what is going on in the world of culture still has to pay great attention to what is going on in Europe. The cultural balance, like the political and the economic balance, has certainly swung our way, but it is a balance, and no contrast between everything and nothing. What the historian of ideas will eventually make of Existentialism we cannot know. But it is surely the most important philosophical movement since the war, and it is essentially European—German and French—in origin. In the fine arts, in music, in literature, in the lesser arts, European names still fill the pages of the critical journals all over the world. Our age may be degenerate, Alexandrian or worse, but we are all Alexandrians together in the West. We Americans cannot claim absolute domination, not even as hopeless neurotics, or materialists, or makers of the wastelands of the soul.

One more word before I leave the intellectuals. An American who moves about in intellectual circles in Western Europe is, unless he is much more thick-skinned than we usually are, bound to feel uncomfortable. These people make little effort to disguise the fact that they distrust and fear the United States. There are quite obvious reasons why they feel this way. They have directly suffered the

ravages of war, and we have not. They envy our obvious
prosperity. They resent the patronizing attitude many
Americans abroad all too often assume. They resent, being
only human, our very generosity toward them. They are
afraid we are about to enter the kind of career of expansion
their own history has shown that great victorious nations
have so often entered. Above all, I think, since they are
intellectuals who prize the traditional refinements, they
tend to think of us as essentially vulgar and tasteless, as, if
I may speak symbolically, about to force upon them
Coca-Cola and destroy their wines.

All this comes out neatly in a postwar German novel by
Maria von Kirchbach, called *Cupid in Khaki.* Its heroine,
whose husband has been made prisoner of war, is besieged
by an American officer in the forces of occupation. He
offers her all the riches of the Post Exchange, all the little
luxuries she has had so long to do without. She is sorely
tempted, but it is fair to say that her tempter behaves quite
honorably, for an American. At the right moment, the
husband comes back from Russian captivity, and the wife,
putting European spirituality and *douceur de vivre* ahead
of crass American materialism, decides to stay with her
husband. This attitude, even among the most aesthetically
inclined, is not without its amusing ambivalence, for the
very same ones who declare we are all Babbitts or worse
also have the greatest respect for Hemingway and Faulkner,
even for Steinbeck and Damon Runyan. Part of the trouble
is that they suffer from cultural lag. European intellectuals
tend to think of the United States as our own intellectuals
thought of it in the 1920's. They are still back with
Sinclair Lewis and Mr. H. L. Mencken. We ourselves are

thus not altogether without responsibility for their opinion of us. Time, we may hope, will remedy this lag.

Many American liberals are so hostile to nationalism—except among colonial peoples—and so distrustful of the commonplaces of nationalism in general, that they will not face the obvious. But it seems inescapably true, as such analogies go, that we feel very differently about criticism from within the family and from without. We take what Sinclair Lewis and Mr. Mencken, what Mr. Lewis Mumford and Miss Hortense Powdermaker have to say about our crudities in our stride, but we bristle when an Englishman or a Frenchman says the same things. This is a fact of life, a law of nature, and the best we can do is allow for it. We can indeed try to see that Europeans learn about our good points as well as about our bad ones, and this our State Department is trying hard to do, under heavy fire from within the country, as it always is.

Our propaganda—for such it is—runs among European intellectuals up against their preconceived notions of the United States as a vast Hollywood, and against their distrust of all propaganda not directly stamped by the tradition of intellectual revolt. Their attitude is hard for us to understand sympathetically, but we must make the effort. After all, I must repeat, they are simply saying what our own intellectuals said about us a generation ago, and what some of them are still saying.

Politically this distrust of the United States takes among the West European intellectual classes rather the form of "neutralism" than that of actual siding with Russia against us. The neutralist feels like Mercutio, victim of the struggle between Montagues and Capulets—"a plague o' both your houses." It is not a noble feeling, nor has it a sound logical basis in history. The spiritual crisis of our age has roots in Western Europe at least as deep as in the United States and Russia. Most reflective Europeans know this quite well. But the war was fought there, not here, and we should realize that Mercutio's response is a most human one. Some of us Americans have made this response even today, and it looks in the perspective of history as if Americans collectively made a very similar response in 1919, when we were quite willing to abandon all Europe to its Montagues and Capulets.

Nor should we close our minds to the possibility that European neutralism, *in its milder and more sensible forms*, may be a force for good in our divided world. The concept of an honest broker, a mediator between the two extremes, is one many Americans, in the midst of this coldhot war, find most unpalatable. We don't need an umpire —this is no game. But in calmer moments we may bring ourselves to admit that not all compromise is appeasement. Here the Western Europeans, working within the United Nations, may yet help bring about a new and more satisfactory Locarno. There *is* a difference between compromise and appeasement, however tricky that distinction may seem to the confirmed semanticist, and the Europeans are perhaps better placed than we are to help bring that difference out concretely.

The ordinary man, as I have already suggested, does not altogether reflect the dislike and distrust of the United States common, though by no means universal, among European intellectuals. He may, and if he is a Communist he certainly does, fear us as a possible aggressor. But he does not share the intellectual's distrust of our material

achievements. Indeed, he would like to have some of them
for himself. I do not think he has taken overly much to
Coca-Cola, but he would certainly like a Chevrolet, or a
television set, or a house with all the latest improvements.
And, to the horror of the intellectuals, he seems to like
American movies. Indeed, I think it fair to say that the
European man in the street looks at us with admiration
mixed with envy. But it is not a searing envy, not indeed
a hopeless envy, and my net impression is that on the whole
he thinks quite a lot better of us than of the Russians. This,
as I shall shortly point out, is confirmed by the pollers of
public opinion.

Our real interest in the average Western European,
however, should be in his feelings about his own prospects
and the future of his society. The man in the street has
opinions, and ultimately in all these societies can if he
votes together in a mass swing the fate of Western Europe.
He need not vote, indeed, but only acquiesce. It is rather
more than a half-truth—perhaps a four-fifths truth—that a
people gets the government it wants, or perhaps deserves.
If the European masses are apathetic, resigned to sullen
submission, unwilling to work, quietly desperate, then they
are headed for dictatorship of the Right. If they are actively
indignant at what they think the injustice of the ruling
classes, if they feel an explosive hatred toward the government, if they are also full of energy, they are headed
toward a revolution which I think in these days can only
lead to dictatorship of the Left.

Yet the state of mind of the average man is hard to test
objectively. The mere traveler's impressions must always
be suspect, and the formal study of public opinion is, as
a social science, still in its beginnings. Yet there are promis-

ing beginnings. The systematic study of the press, inter-
views with escaped Europeans, the cautious use of cloak-
and-dagger sources, together with a good background
knowledge of the societies studied, enabled the Americans
and the British to estimate with surprising accuracy the
way their armies would be received on the continent in
1944. To such sources the professional student of public
opinion can now add the public-opinion polls. These polls,
which incidentally would appear to be part of our American
contribution to the culture of the West, now exist in most
of the countries of free Europe and are federated into a
World Association for Public Opinion Research. In many
circles it is fashionable to sneer at the pollsters, but I think
no one conscientiously interested in the truth about human
behavior on this earth can afford such a sneer. Most of these
research workers are aware that a scientist would indeed
be a faker if he made no mistakes.

I shall here confine myself to a few mere scraps of
testing from France, which after all does seem to be the
country most seared by the horrors of our time. *Sondages*
("Samplings" or "Soundings"), the organ of the Institut
Français d'Opinion Publique, a very active group in
French academic life, is a fascinating record of French
public opinion on most varied subjects. Its polls are
sharpest, perhaps, when concentrated on questions of political measures, domestic and international, but it also
goes on to wider if vaguer questions of man's fate. In
1951, for example, *Sondages* conducted a poll on private
worries, and discovered the not surprising fact that more
people worried—or admitted worrying—about money than
about any other single matter. But in a breakdown by
classes, the well-to-do in October 1949 showed 33 per cent

worrying most about money, the middle class 52 per cent, the lower middle class 63 per cent, the poor 63 per cent. Americans with stereotypes about France may be surprised to learn that worrying about love affairs, which was not even separately listed, but buried among "personal and health problems," could achieve in September 1951 only a second place of 10 per cent. "Uncertainty about the future" could do no better than tie for fifth place with 6 per cent. But these soundings are likely to be destructive of our simpler stereotypes about the French. A study of opinion about Paris, both among Parisians and provincials, is full of interesting details. I note that in the provinces 30 per cent admitted envying their relatives or friends in Paris, but 65 per cent stated that they did not envy them. Of course, they may have been lying, the curse of all these polls; but I have always suspected the notion that every Frenchman would live in Paris if he could. I can mention but one more detail, a French poll of August 1950, after the outbreak of the Korean War. There were in sympathy with the United States 52 per cent, in sympathy with Russia 13 per cent. You may wonder about the remaining 35 per cent. Well, 18 per cent "ne se prononcent pas," do not answer, a not surprising percentage in a question as sharp as this, and 17 per cent made "other responses," which I guess to have been variations on Mercutio's "a plague o' both your houses."

We cannot linger any longer over these details, which I suggest add up to an alert, active, disputatious people, but not to one on the verge of a collective nervous breakdown. We may take it as typical of the characteristic French diversity of opinion that 30 per cent of parents polled were for compulsory Latin for their children, 28 per cent were against it, and 42 per cent were in a position that suggests to me that French parents are weakening, getting Americanized—they were "undecided."

Sport deserves a serious word. There is no good sociology of sport, no doubt because those who know most about sociology know little about sport, and those who know most about sport know little about sociology. But Americans in particular, if they are not intellectuals, are likely to estimate athletic achievement as at least a kind of index of the vitality of a group. Here our national assumption of superiority is pretty complete. Europeans, many of us think, simply can't compete with us. Certainly we always manage, at least by the unofficial point scores our reporters make, to win the Olympic games. But even in sports, the American advantage is only a comparative one. The Europeans manage to hold up their end.

Indeed, in some respects European sport seems in a healthier state than in this country. Their professional sport, like ours, exists to make money for its promoters, to give the public a chance to gamble, and by no means just incidentally, to satisfy the pride, the pooled self-esteem, of a group, local, regional, or national. Neither the purely commercial side, nor the gambling side, nor the gladiatorial side—the subsidized few playing for the amusement of the many spectators—of professional sports are very different in Western Europe from what they are in this country. It is, however, in amateur sport that the West Europeans seem today, on the whole, rather nearer the conventional ideals of sport for sport's sake, of widespread actual play, than we do. Golf is far less popular, save perhaps in Britain, than here. Tennis, on the other hand, is played a great deal in Western Europe. Amateur team sports in Europe have never been as closely identified with higher education as in America. Soccer, which is for Europeans what baseball is for us, rugby, field hockey, basketball, and in Britain alone, cricket, are all played by innumerable clubs organized specifically for play, and identified with a great variety of neighborhood, vocational, class, even religious groups. One result is that the West European young man does not stop team play at twenty-one or twenty-two when he graduates from college, and content himself with golf, tennis, or squash thereafter. He keeps right on with his club, often well into middle age.

European nationalism finds a steady outlet in sport. The neutral spectator at an international soccer match between France and Germany, say—relations were resumed in 1952 with France winning the first match—may well doubt whether such contests do in fact lessen national antagonisms. Certainly he will take in a somewhat ironic sense the notion that international team sports fulfill William James's call for a "moral equivalent of war." Yet here as so often the idealist asks for too much. To judge by the behavior of the crowds—and the writings of sports reporters afterward—a good deal of what in present-day cant terms is called "aggression" does get taken out in ways much less violent than actual warfare. International sport as it now is in Western Europe may not be an effective sublimation of aggressive drives; but it is at least a partial satisfaction—since even the little countries can sometimes beat the big ones at soccer—of the pooled self-esteem of nationalism.

Perhaps it is just as well that, except for the Olympic games, which come only once in four years, and tennis, which remains pretty genteel in spite of the crowd appeal of Davis Cup matches, we Americans do not compete with

Europeans on a national basis in team sports with mass spectators. Our national drive in such activities would doubtless push us to the top rather too much of the time for a Europe that likes to have the spoils well shared. As it is, we go on playing among ourselves alone our peculiar kind of football, in which foot and ball meet with increasing rareness; and we play baseball with no more international competition than that afforded by an occasional Japanese or Caribbean team. Of course, it would take us some time to polish up our soccer, and practically learn rugby and cricket, in order to compete with European countries in these sports, and at first we might be soundly beaten—something that in Bentham's terms would certainly bring the greatest happiness to the greatest number. For there is no doubt that the ordinary European, if he does not hate us as do some intellectuals, is a bit tired of our eternal successes.

Still, as one looks over the complex activities men label "sport," the likenesses, the identities indeed, between Americans and Western Europeans stand out perhaps even more sharply than they do in what we commonly think of as higher forms of culture. A fan is a fan everywhere, even in England, where if cricket crowds are decorous, soccer crowds are not. But the easy test is the journalism of sport, which shows but slightly the stamp of national character. Sports writers everywhere go in for elegant variation, pumped-up drama, and critical attitudes which suggest that most of them, in France and Britain as in the United States, are good sound intellectuals and should have columns of their own. If there is a difference in man playing in the United States and in Western Europe, it is slight, very slight, and sociologically not really important. It is tempting to find Europeans at play a little less tense than we are, a little less

painfully self-conscious heirs of Hercules, a little more serene. Europeans, and especially Frenchmen, fish happily
without ever catching a fish, and apparently without ex-
pecting to. We Americans want to catch the legal limit or
a bit more, or get the fish and game commissioner out of
office. Few Frenchmen would even in literature identify
the fisherman with Prometheus, as Melville and Hemingway
do; Loti's *Pêcheur d'Islande* is a quiet fellow indeed beside
Captain Ahab and Hemingway's old man of the sea.

But here again the eternal difficulty of generalization in
such matters crops up. If sport is at one extreme team competition before mass spectators, at the other it is one man or
a few climbing a mountain, diving under the sea, sailing a
raft across the ocean. It is adventure, exploration, the assault
on the unknown—and the breaking of a record. There is
nothing very serene, quiet, or even very sensible, about
most of these activities and a Voltaire or a Shaw has always
had fun with these heaven-stormers. But Heartbreak House
never really understands Horseback Hall. The most con-
secrated of sportmen, the mountain climbers, are almost
always themselves intellectuals, members of Heartbreak
House. In our Western tradition, the adventurer, the ex-
plorer, *le recordman* (the word unbelievably is French), is
surely associated with life, with the Promethean spark. In
these days of Everest and Annapurna, of the Kon-Tiki
expedition, and many more instances of man struggling
heroically if not without publicity against fate, Europe
would seem to be very much alive indeed, more alive than
we are. But these are honors we may well leave to the
Europeans. After all, we Americans allowed the adven-
turous French and Spaniards to explore the interior of
North America; we merely peopled it.

I should like to conclude with what I regard as decisive

evidence that the peoples of Western Europe are not losing
their hold on life. Back in the 1930's the demographers were
sure the population curve in Western Europe and in the
United States was flattening out. Now they know that
there was immediately after the war a sharp rise in the birth
rate, a rise certainly far greater than the normal postwar rise
from postponed marriages and return of husbands, and not
really anticipated by the experts.

A final statistical table is called for here. The source is
the *Demographic Yearbook, 1952* (Statistical Office of the
United Nations, New York, 1952, pp. 224–231).

Table 3.   Crude Birth Rates

	1937	*1949*
Austria	12.8	16.3
Belgium	15.4	17.2
Denmark	18.0	18.9
France	15.0	20.9
Ireland	19.2	21.5
Italy	22.9	20.4
Netherlands	19.8	23.7
Norway	15.0	19.5
Spain	22.7	21.7
United Kingdom	15.3	17.0
United States	17.1	24.0

The curve is now flattening out a bit, but we are still far
from the rates of the 1930's over most of Western society.
Now I see no way you can account for all these babies
except by giving up a position of extreme pessimism as to
the temper of the parents. One European intellectual with
whom I discussed this point did indeed argue that the rise
in birth rate is a sign of despair; people no longer give a
damn, they are sunk in sensuality, and anyway the welfare
state will take care of the children. Surely this assertion is
almost a caricature of the intellectual's unwillingness to get

beyond what his emotions dictate to his deductive proc-
esses. If you incline, as so many of our supposedly anti-
Marxists do, to the economic interpretation of human mo-
tivation, you will say that we are in prosperous times—even
in dying Western Europe—and that of course the birth rate
rises. But this is at least an admission that we *are* in prosperous times. If you incline to Freudian or similar psychological interpretations, you may say that this generation has
come to feel that contraception is unduly repressive and
inhibiting, that the one-child family is cruelty to the only
child, that at least two or three children are necessary for
the parents' ids, libidos, or just plain human nature. If you
incline to put great emphasis on the postwar revival of religious orthodoxy and moral seriousness, you have still another
explanation for the rise in the birth rate. You may, if you
like hard-boiled simplicity, say that we have large families
in the middle classes just because our parents had small
ones. If you believe that in such great social phenomena
we must always deal with multiple causation, you may say
that all these explanations, and others we have not touched
upon, are factors in the end result. You will not, however,
find it easy to explain this renewal of life as in itself a sure
sign of approaching death.

We come at the end of this study by no means to the
unfashionable—and unsound—conclusion that this is the
best of possible worlds in Western Europe. On the contrary, we know that Europeans are facing heavy burdens
and difficult problems. But we know, first, what I have
throughout rather implied by occasional cross-references
to the United States than brought out explicitly, that these
burdens and these problems are not limited to Western
Europe, but are basically shared with us; they are the

common burdens and problems of the free Western world, from which we Americans are by no means exempt. And we know, second, that Europeans are for the most part not laying down the burdens and dodging the problems, but are facing their future with courage and resourcefulness. My slanting reference immediately above to Dr. Pangloss's optimism about the "best of possible worlds" carries my incurably historical imagination back to his creator. Voltaire's *Candide* is a bitter satire, and his hero's woes could hardly have been greater in our century than in his own. Yet in the end, you will remember, Candide decides that "il faut cultiver notre jardin"—we must cultivate our garden. This the Europeans are now doing. It is still a fine garden, and they are still good gardeners.

I would not, however, end on so subdued a note. There is resignation, acceptance of this world in Western Europe, but there is also the lift of courage and hope. Honegger, the French composer, by origin a Swiss, was one of those Parisians who cultivated their gardens through the gloomy months after the fall of France in 1940. His "Symphony for String Orchestra" was finished in the autumn of 1941. It is a quiet work—quiet certainly for the composer of "Pacific 231" and "Rugby"—perhaps a bit remote, and not an obvious program piece. But at the very end of the last movement, the trumpets, hitherto silent and unnoticed as the strings play on, burst suddenly into a simple and very moving chorale. I cannot think of a Voltairian chorale, nor indeed of an Existentialist chorale. Honegger's trumpets called in that year of Nazi triumph to something deeper and older in the human spirit than anything the mere social scientist can put into words. They are still calling, still heard. You can hear them, if you will, even above the very great noise the prophets of doom are making.